THE NATURAL ADVANTAGE

HOW MORE TIME OUTSIDE
REDUCES STRESS, IMPROVES HEALTH
& BOOSTS SOCIAL CONNECTION

DR JENNY BROCKIS

MAJOR STREET

THE
NATURAL
ADVANTAGE

HOW MORE TIME OUTSIDE
REDUCES STRESS, IMPROVES HEALTH
& BOOSTS SOCIAL CONNECTION

DR JENNY BROCKIS

Praise for *The Natural Advantage*

"Dr Jenny Brockis has, once again, masterfully distilled extensive international research into a reader-friendly guide, rich with actionable insights. With an engaging style, Dr Brockis pairs ancestral wisdom with cutting edge science, leaving the reader with no doubt about the connections between nature and human well-being. Framed by the author's own deep connection to the natural world, the discoveries shared in *The Natural Advantage* affirm Dr Brockis' international status as a trusted authority on the science of lifestyle medicine"
Alan C. Logan, co-author of *Your Brain, on Nature*

"This book is a brilliant and concise summary about all that's wrong with modern life – and more importantly, what we need to do about it to restore balance in the modern world through the biopsychosocial model of health. It's based on cutting-edge science, is easy to read and gives clear guidance on concrete actions that you can take today and tomorrow to improve your life. I highly recommend that you buy this book, implement the strategies and then enjoy the fruits of your labour for the rest of your life."
Paul Taylor, exercise physiologist, nutritionist, neuroscientist, podcaster and author of *Death by Comfort*

"In *The Natural Advantage*, Jenny offers an insightful exploration of our innate connection to nature and the health and lifestyle benefits of this connection. She explores the evidence for these benefits, illuminated by stories from her own life and shows that regardless of where we live, we can all do something to harness these benefits. The link to lifestyle medicine adds weight to the argument for including time spent in nature as another fundamental pillar of thriving health and well-being.
If you want to learn more about the health benefits that might be, quite literally, floating in the air around you, then it's time to read *The Natural Advantage*. In the park, of course."
Simon Matthews FACLM FASLM MHlthSc DipIBLM, psychologist and coach

"Having spent many years diving deep into the researched benefits of nature, it was so refreshing to read a book that articulates these benefits in such a light, fun and engaging way. From the very beginning, I was captivated. Sprinkled with humour and extremely relatable life situations, this book will undoubtedly appeal to a wide audience, especially to those who need it most. It is filled with fascinating facts about the health benefits of nature that keep you engrossed throughout.
Sign me up for #onesmallthing I can do to boost my natural advantage!"
Waminda Parker, co-director and director NatureFix

"*The Natural Advantage* reflects how easy it can be to start with #onesmall thing for positive change. Jenny provides beautifully crafted observations and insights based on science to describe how the sheer simplicity of nature can bring calm to complex lives. This book reminds us that right on our doorsteps (and beyond) are myriad natural opportunities to reduce stress. And Just. Feel. Better. Worth a read. Outside if you can!"
Dominique Mecoy OAM, CEO Leadership WA

"*The Natural Advantage* is extremely accessible and easy to devour. It is like a friendly, personal companion giving you insights and practical tips on how and why nature is essential for relieving our stress in our increasingly chaotic environment. I can now see why digging in my garden puts me in the right frame of mind to deal with the challenges I face as a busy professional in a capital city. I can also appreciate why a run along the water clears my head and lets me be more productive. There are plenty of ideas of how you can bring more nature to city lives to soothe the soul and reduce modern stress for a healthier life."
Monique Zytnik, communication expert and author of *Internal Communication in the Age of Artificial Intelligence*

"This book is a beautiful exploration into the profound impact nature has on our well-being. I love the combination of science and practical tips on how to bring more nature into our lives, and the ideas offer us all a deeper insight into, and connection to, our natural world. This is a must-read for anyone looking to reconnect with nature and enhance their mental and emotional health."
Sue Langley, CEO and founder of The Langley Group

"*The Natural Advantage* by Dr Jenny Brockis is a compelling exploration of how nature can profoundly impact our health and well-being. As a lifestyle medicine physician and 'Doctor Outdoors', I have seen firsthand the transformative effects of incorporating nature into daily life. Dr Brockis brilliantly combines science and practical advice, making this book an essential read for anyone seeking to harness the healing power of the natural world."
Melissa Sundermann, DO, FACOI, DipABLM, FACLM

"In *The Natural Advantage*, Dr Brockis unveils why the closer we are to nature, the happier and healthier we can be. It is a poignant reminder of what's so great about the great outdoors and how we can harness nature's healing and life-enriching powers."
Professor Darren Morton, Director, Lifestyle Medicine and Health Research Centre, Avondale University, Founding Director, The Lift Project and author of *Live More: Happy*

To Julie, Liz and Sue,
for sharing your love of nature with me.

First published in 2024 by Major Street Publishing Pty Ltd
info@majorstreet.com.au | majorstreet.com.au

© Dr Jenny Brockis 2024
The moral rights of the author have been asserted.

 A catalogue record for this book is available from the National Library of Australia

Printed book ISBN: 978-1-923186-19-4
Ebook ISBN: 978-1-923186-20-0

All rights reserved. Except as permitted under *The Australian Copyright Act 1968* (for example, a fair dealing for the purposes of study, research, criticism or review), no part of this book may be reproduced, stored in a retrieval system, communicated or transmitted in any form or by any means without prior written permission. All inquiries should be made to the publisher.

Cover design by Typography Studio
Internal design by Production Works

10 9 8 7 6 5 4 3 2 1

Disclaimer

The material in this publication is in the nature of general comment only, and neither purports nor intends to be advice. Readers should not act on the basis of any matter in this publication without considering (and if appropriate taking) professional advice with due regard to their own particular circumstances. The author and publisher expressly disclaim all and any liability to any person, whether a purchaser of this publication or not, in respect of anything and the consequences of anything done or omitted to be done by any such person in reliance, whether whole or partial, upon the whole or any part of the contents of this publication.

Contents

Acknowledgments ix
Introduction: Time to unpack your natural advantage 1

PART I | Reconnecting with nature: what do you need to attend to? 25

Chapter 1	Sight	27
Chapter 2	Hearing	39
Chapter 3	Smell and taste	51
Chapter 4	Body	65
Chapter 5	Mind	76
Chapter 6	Soul	88

PART II | Nature's medicine 115

Chapter 7	Air	117
Chapter 8	Sunshine	128
Chapter 9	Water	140
Chapter 10	Earth	155
Chapter 11	Animals	160

Conclusion: Your nature prescription 169
About the author 177
References 178

Acknowledgments

First, my sincere thanks go to Lesley Williams, Will Allen and the rest of the team at Major Street Publishing for believing in this book and working with me to make it a reality.

Writing this book would not have been possible without the inspiration, wisdom and research of those who have taught me so much. I am deeply grateful to have had the opportunity to learn from the work of Florence Williams, Alan Logan and Eva Selhub, Qing Li, Avery Clemens, Yoshifumi Miyazaki, Xiaoqi Feng, Wallace J Nichols, Thomas Astell-Burt, Richard Strayer, David L Strayer, Richard Louv, Robin Wall Kimmerer and Bonnie Tsui, to name just a few, who awakened my insight into just how powerful time in nature is for our health and well-being.

My introduction to lifestyle medicine eight years ago rekindled my passion for medicine. The healthcare system we have been operating under is long overdue a reset, and I firmly believe this will happen through the acceptance and implementation of lifestyle medicine principles that seek to inspire complete health and well-being based on sound scientific evidence – promoting good health by addressing the causes of disease and seeking to integrate positive and healthy behaviours that keep us well. I am indebted to all my lifestyle medicine colleagues and friends who inspire me every day to do more.

My curiosity to learn led me to undertake the 'Wellbeing Inspired by Nature' course run by Geeta Stilwell and Manuela Siegfried. Thank you both for sharing your wisdom and ideas. I learned so much.

Thank you to my literary friends Sue and Liz for your willingness to peruse the initial manuscript in its earliest format and provide unfettered feedback to help shape the book.

Thank you to all of those who volunteered to share their stories of how nature has positively impacted your lives. I'm so grateful for your generosity and vulnerability in doing so.

Thank you also to my wonderful friend and book coach, Kelly Irving. Being part of your Expert Author Community has been such a gift, Kelly. Your love for what you do permeates every drop of your being as you encourage and challenge us all to write better.

Scott Eathorne, publicist extraordinaire, I can't believe this is the third time we have worked together. Thank you so much, my friend, for your ability to get my books seen by the wider world.

Thank you to all my friends and colleagues who quietly ask, 'How's the book going, Jenny?' Your support means so much.

Lastly, I want to express my gratitude to my husband, John, who has now had to put up with several periods of time when, in book-writing mode, I squirrel myself in my study for weeks on end. You've always supported my efforts and never questioned my need for space and quiet to do my deep work. I love you so much.

Introduction
Time to unpack your natural advantage

'For someone living with high-functioning anxiety, you've made some interesting career choices.'

Whoa! This statement from my psychologist hit me like a thunderbolt. I'm a person with what?

I had always joked that anxiety was my middle name. It had been my constant companion through medical school, while working as a GP, and then as a corporate public speaker. I had always treated my anxiety as part of who I was, something I battled every day to ensure I could keep up with my studies, pass all the exams and learn how to speak confidently on a stage in front of hundreds of people.

Until then, I had never considered it something I didn't have to live with. I had reconciled myself to only being anxiety-free on those short breaks far away from the hustle and noise of the daily grind, when I escaped to those places where I could truly relax and be myself. My many trips to quiet and remote places, taking walks to clear my head and getting outside into the sunshine, had always made me feel better.

Suddenly, it all made sense. I'd had the solution to my stress and anxiety all along but had remained blind to it. As Melo Calarco says in his book *Beating Burnout, Finding Balance*, 'You can't change what you don't notice'.

Chronic stress – our biggest blind spot

Have you ever wondered why in our modern world, where we have so much going for us with new technologies, AI, rapid advancements in medical treatments and access to clean running water and healthy food, so many of us are struggling with chronically high stress levels? Whether it's excessive noise, getting caught in traffic, having to deal with unreasonable clients, getting another speeding ticket, or worrying about meeting a deadline when you're so far behind, there is much going on that causes us stress. Our daily hassles, inconveniences and worries continue to pile up and grind us down.

One survey found that 60% of respondents across 34 countries felt stressed to the point they couldn't cope at least once in the past year, while 39% admitted their level of stress meant they had to take time off work.

Modern life is stressful. Its fast pace, high pressure and steep expectations contribute to bone-numbing fatigue and the question of when this will ever end. But it's not just making us feel overwhelmed and exhausted – it's making us sick. It's increasing our risk of physical illness, including headaches, stomach ulcers and heart disease, and it's increasing our risk of psychological distress, mental illness and burnout.

Unresolved chronic stress is leading to greater anxiety and other mental health challenges. It is causing poorer physical health and increasing the burden of chronic disease. It is driving a wedge into our society, adding to our loss of connection, creating more loneliness, contributing to the rise of unprovoked anger and violence, and polarising communities.

Have we lost sight of our humanity – to be kind and compassionate, and to care about each other? Have we created a nightmare world?

One in seven Australian adults is taking antidepressants. At the same time, the growing levels of anxiety in our children, sometimes impacting their ability to attend regular school, are worrying many parents and healthcare practitioners. The concern is that the next generation won't be able to handle the demands, rapid changes and uncertainties of the future.

The statistics themselves make for depressing reading. According to the Australian Bureau of Statistics, one in five people (21.5% of the adult population) are living with a diagnosed mental health disorder, and for the majority (17.2%) that disorder is anxiety.

And that's just those who have sought help. There are probably many more living with mental health challenges who have chosen not to seek help for whatever reason – shame, embarrassment, guilt, stigma or the fact that they don't think they are unwell enough to need help.

A cross-analysis of population surveys of 156,331 people aged 18 and over from 29 countries showed that half the population can expect to have had a mental health disorder by age 75 years, with the average age of onset being 15 years. These are the ones I worry about the most – the 38.8% of individuals aged 16 to 24 already living with a diagnosed mental disorder. More worrying still is the fact that anxiety and phobias start to be diagnosed from the age of five and a half. That is not a typo.

The paradox of stress

We evolved with stress. A bit of stress works wonders to give us a reason to get out of bed in the morning, prepare us to deal with the day's challenges and, above all, keep us safe. Our highly efficient fight, flight or freeze response enabled us throughout our evolution to recognise if we were in a place of potential danger and take the appropriate steps to escape.

If stress is your friend by helping you step up to a challenge and focus on what you need to do next, how come it's created muscular tension so tight across your shoulders that you're worried you'll snap like an overtightened violin string? Why, ladies, does your level of premenstrual tension regularly change you into a snarling pit bull at certain times of the month? And why, gentlemen, are you no longer the relaxed, handsome Mr Darcys emerging from a quick dip in the pool but snorting, snappy balls of anger and frustration ready to pick a fight?

Keeping our stress within a tolerable or optimal zone allows us to function at our best and sustainably. The problem is that in developed countries, stress levels are rising faster than sea levels, and our chronic exposure to multiple stressors is harming us.

It's like the story of Goldilocks and the three bears, but about stress and not porridge – too little stress makes us feel apathetic and bored, while too much leads to exhaustion, burnout and illness.

Today's busy lives mean you're likely to be dealing with multiple stressors, many of which cannot be resolved easily, quickly or at all. This leaves you exhausted and constantly on the lookout for what might happen next. At the all-you-can-eat stress buffet, it can be hard not to pile up your plate with far more stress than you can reasonably handle.

Beyond overwork, the kids giving you grief and the financial stress of surviving the rising cost of everything, one of the biggest stressors is insufficient or poor sleep. What's your sleep pattern like? Can you remember the last time you slept well and woke up fresh as a daisy in the morning? What with the kids and the dog all wanting to come and join you in bed at night, a partner who snores like a wild wildebeest, and a brain that fails to switch off, keeping you in party mode with all your most worrying thoughts circling in your head all night long, sleep can be elusive. Every morning, you wake up tired – and you haven't even gotten out of bed yet.

Maybe you went to bed later than planned because you had a couple of urgent work emails to send and needed to respond to that unpleasant text message from a colleague you have issues with, and then you fell asleep on the couch while watching an episode of you can't remember what on Netflix. The next morning, you're not your best shiny self. You're a little bit sluggish, brain-fogged and slugging coffee like it's about to be abolished.

Poor sleep due to stress affects your ability to regulate your emotions. Stress narrows your cognitive bandwidth, meaning you can only handle one thing at a time, you're not open to new ideas, and you don't want your colleague coming by all cheery and suggesting things to help that you don't want to hear. You find yourself crying over the photocopier when the paper gets jammed (again). You're behind, overwhelmed and stressed to the eyeballs, thinking that there's no way you'll get home on time tonight, and who will be cooking dinner?

Too much chronic stress causes levels of the stress hormone cortisol to stay too high. Usually, it ebbs and flows throughout your day, peaking in the morning to help you wake up and then declining. Over time, too much cortisol becomes toxic:

- It inhibits neuroplasticity, your brain's ability to rewire and adapt to changing circumstances, create new memories and help you learn. You can't think straight, you keep forgetting things, you're easily fazed by things going wrong, your sleep is fragmented, and you're putting on so much weight (especially around your belly) despite trying to exercise more and eat more healthily.

- It inhibits neurogenesis, your brain's ability to produce new neurons.
- It's normal for our brains to shrink a little as we age, but this occurs more quickly when cortisol levels are chronically high.
- It leads to a state of chronic low-level inflammation, which puts you at risk of developing illness or disease.

It's important to distinguish between short-term inflammation due to injury or infection, like an ingrown toenail, and systemic low-grade inflammation that develops due to exposure to chronic stress. With your ingrown toenail, you'll notice how the affected part feels warm to the touch, and the surrounding skin looks red, swollen and painful. This is because your body has mustered its troops – a range of pro-inflammatory cytokines produced by your immune cells – to attack and get rid of the bacterial invaders. However, in chronic stress, these pro-inflammatory cytokines go into overdrive, attacking healthy tissue and organs, and potentially triggering autoimmune diseases such as rheumatoid arthritis and lupus.

Chronic low-level inflammation is associated with many chronic diseases, including:

- heart disease
- inflammatory bowel disease
- chronic obstructive pulmonary disease (COPD) and asthma
- depression

- type 2 diabetes
- Alzheimer's disease
- Parkinson's disease
- some cancers.

If too much stress is harming us mentally and physically, it's time to examine what has contributed to it and how to manage it effectively.

How our environment contributes to stress

New York and Tokyo were the world's first megacities, each reaching a population of 10 million in the 1950s. Today, more than half the world's population lives in a city, and this is projected to rise to 68% by 2050.

We have had cities since Mesopotamian times, 3000 BC, but humans have only moved to cities en masse in the last couple of centuries, mostly to look for work as we moved from a predominantly agrarian culture to an industrialised one.

Urban living has many benefits, and many people love city life, but there are also some downsides. Traffic congestion, air pollution and noise are not only annoying, they are also bad for our health. In some areas, poor urban planning has created concrete jungles that are heat traps, causing the urban heat island effect. With climate change a reality, while we can crank up the air conditioning to help, this is not a sustainable solution. Neither can we expect to alleviate the high stress associated with modern living with the occasional weekend off or digital detox.

As cities grow, so too do the inequities. A 2008 Lancet study of 40 million Britons found a link between income inequality, access to green spaces and life expectancy. How much you earn in rural areas has little impact on life expectancy, but city dwellers with the lowest incomes have a ten-year-lower life expectancy than the richest, who live in the open, leafy suburbs. Urban overcrowding, poor living conditions and difficulty finding work or earning enough to pay the bills create stress and increase the risk of poor health and mental illness.

But there's something else. Have you felt it, too? We've become increasingly disconnected from the natural world.

Every generation has probably said they were the last to play outside, but how we spend our leisure and recreation time has changed dramatically as TV, smartphones and video games have become more widely available. Some of today's city kids have never visited a farm, collected eggs from a chicken coop or patted a horse, nor do they know what an eggplant is.

Crowded work schedules take up more of our time, reducing the time available to go to a park or participate in outdoor activities. Not only do we visit parks less often, but we spend less time there when we do. More and more, we experience nature only through a screen. We have become not just city dwellers but indoor dwellers, encased in our homes and offices, travelling in cars on our asphalt roads, flying in silver tubes, and rarely venturing outside.

You may be shocked to know that the average adult currently spends between 95% and 98% of their awake time inside. How can this be possible? Let's look at what a regular day looks like to you.

Whether you live in a house or apartment, if you have work to get to, you'll likely travel there by car, bus or train. Do you get into your vehicle in the garage and use the garage door remote to get outside? If you can access a company car park, is this underground, multistorey or open?

Then, how much of your working day do you spend sitting at your desk indoors?

After making dinner and catching up on your kids' and partners' day, do you now spend time supervising homework, doing the laundry, getting ready for tomorrow and phoning your parents to ensure they're doing OK? If you're exhausted or have work to catch up on, will you really get out to exercise?

We spend remarkably little time outside, let alone noticing what's around us. You may even be afraid to venture outside, especially when it's dark.

City dwellers are 56% more at risk of experiencing major depression, mood disorders or anxiety. It's not that urban life itself causes more stress – though sometimes it can feel that way – but rather that natural environments assist you in lowering your stress.

Living with too much stress from too much work, too much time inside, too much time interacting with our technology rather than each other, and the false belief that the only way to achieve success (whatever your definition of success looks like) is always to work harder and for longer than everyone else is not sustainable.

Introducing biophilia

Going to see your health practitioner when unwell often results in you getting a prescription to speed your recovery. If you ever leave empty-handed, do you sometimes feel a bit… cheated? Being told that all your tests are normal and there's nothing 'wrong', while reassuring, is frustrating because you are left with unanswered questions as to why you're not feeling good.

It may surprise you to know that medical care accounts for only 10% to 20% of health outcomes. The remaining 80% to 90% result from what the World Health Organization (WHO) defines as the social determinants of health, which include where you live, the work you do, your age, your race, your level of education and your socio-economic status. Many of our chronic diseases are tied to unhealthy lifestyle behaviours and stress. Ultimately, many factors contribute to poor health, and not all of them can be 'fixed' with medication.

When training to become a doctor, I was immersed in learning the intricacies of how the human body works. I was fascinated by how clever it all was and how it was all interconnected.

It used to be believed that the blood-brain barrier caused the head and body to operate independently of each other. How wrong we were. Today, we think of the blood-brain barrier as a highly selective filter keeping the brain safe from harmful substances or pathogens.

Traditionally, western medicine has focused on physiological and psychological needs, but the biopsychosocial (BPS) model (see figure 1) offers a far more holistic view by adopting a whole-person approach, incorporating interpersonal factors.

It's not a new concept, but it has taken time to be fully recognised. The BPS model highlights the interconnectedness of its three aspects. When one part of the triad is disrupted, it has a ripple effect on the others. The social-environmental aspect, which encompasses our interactions with others and our natural world, is a crucial but often overlooked component of this model.

This is where lifestyle medicine practitioners start by unpacking the social determinants that may be involved and guiding you to a better outcome, shifting your behaviours towards including helpful activities in your daily routine, including time in nature. A nature prescription recommends that you get outside and enjoy the great outdoors. It may be a written prescription, verbal counselling, an addition to a chronic disease or mental health care plan, or a referral to a specific provider.

Figure 1: The biopsychosocial model

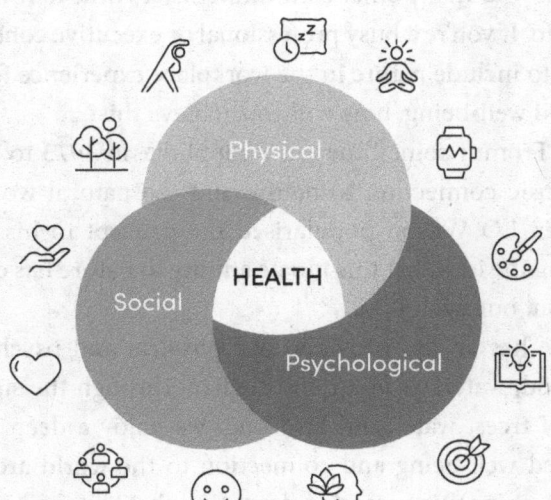

Health is far more than the absence of disease. A vital contributor to staying well, reducing the risk of disease, improving and hastening recovery and enjoying long-term well-being at every age is positive human experience – things that provide us joy, happiness and a sense of connection. While studying positive psychology, I felt as if the curtains had been lifted. I now understand why, in times of trouble, I have always been drawn to spend time, often alone, in nature.

According to Richard Louv, author of *Last Child in the Woods*, we have created a 'nature deficit'. In our busy lives, we spend so much time overthinking, overcommitting and generally overdoing stuff that we have precious little time left, if any, to press pause and reflect on what would help the most to calm our minds and provide the headspace to think things through and feel good.

If you love being outside but never seem to get there anymore because of your many other commitments, it's time to revisit what you can do. If you're a busy professional or executive conscious of the need to include nature in the workplace experience for better health and well-being, how will you achieve this?

Erich Fromm coined the term 'biophilia' in 1973 to describe our intrinsic connection to nature and the natural world. Five years later, EO Wilson popularised the concept in his writing, expanding the idea that this innate affinity to nature has occurred throughout our evolution.

Nature has always provided our physical and psychological needs: food, water, clean air and shelter. Through the sights and sounds of trees, water and birdsong, we enjoy a deep sense of heightened well-being and connection to the world around us. This creates a positive emotional reaction that is stronger in some than others.

Our busy lives create great stress. However, this book will show you how reconnecting with the natural world can counteract the negative effects of too much stress and enhance your cognition (your ability to think), focus and ability to regulate your emotions, boosting creativity and performance. It can also provide the physical benefits of improved cardiovascular health, increased physical fitness, lower inflammation and improved immune function. There's much to gain from a greater connection to nature and so much to lose if we fail to correct our nature deficit.

The idea of using nature to enhance your health and well-being, alleviate some of your stress, reduce the burden of living with chronic illness and alleviate some of your fears, anxieties and sadness may feel too simplistic. But as Leonardo da Vinci said, 'Simplicity is the ultimate sophistication'.

As you explore this book, you'll find some simple ideas which, if they appeal and you are willing to try them, you'll benefit from.

The great awakening

Sometimes it can take a jolt to the system to force us to step back and take stock of how we're living our lives and how that makes us feel. The arrival of the global pandemic and the enforced lockdowns did exactly that, as my friend Michelle described those early days of great uncertainty:

> Thinking back to March 27th 2020, it was about ten days after the borders closed, and we were all ordered home. The (business) phone had stopped ringing, and the emails had stopped arriving. I remember crunching numbers and trying to work out how long we could sustain the business without any income. I remember trawling through my mind for experiences that might help me navigate this one and coming up incredibly short. In my mind, the whole world as I knew it had stopped and changed irrevocably, and I couldn't be sure that we would all be OK.
>
> It was then that I looked out the window and paid attention to what had been happening outside. I noticed the birds and their babies in the nest in the tree.
>
> They had been there all along, but I hadn't seen them until now. Ahh, the whole world hadn't changed.
>
> Everything would be OK.

Many others like Michelle shared similar stories with me of how, during the global pandemic, they found great reassurance in seeing the natural world continuing with business as usual, of seeing the seasons change and new growth heralding the arrival of spring.

Estimates have found that 4.4 billion people, or 57% of the planet's population, were under some form of movement restriction on 5 April 2020. Air traffic decreased by 75%, and driving decreased by more than 40%.

Researchers examining the impact of this cessation of human activity on nature found that, in many instances, nature thrived. During COVID-19, that dark time of our history, the planet that sustains us was still running normally despite everything. The sun was continuing to rise and set. The grass was still growing. The wind was still blowing. If anything, the birds and the animals enjoyed the temporary lull in human activities that normally disturbed their peace and quiet.

In their book *The Consolation of Nature: Spring in the time of the Coronavirus*, three UK naturalists, Michael McCarthy, Jeremy Mynott and Peter Marren, shared their observations of a glorious UK spring from their different locations in Suffolk, Berkshire and south-west London. The book highlights the heightened nature experience that many of us had in our brief excursions outside our homes or, like Michelle, saw through our windows.

It was as if, for the first time, we witnessed the beauty of the world around us, observed the changing seasons, paused to notice the trees, plants and flowers, and remembered how good it was to get outside to breathe in fresh air.

Our great awakening reminded us of some things:

- We are part of nature, but nature doesn't owe us anything. If we're not here, nature will continue without us.
- Nature waits for us to remember she is always there to provide a sense of calm, connection and happiness.
- We, as humans, are highly adaptive and can choose our path.

Above all, it reminded us that what's making us sick doesn't necessarily need a pill.

Intuitively, we know nature is good for us, but let's not get lulled into the false sense of 'everyone knows this, so what's the fuss?' In this book, I want to share what science has revealed about how our interactions with nature assist our health and well-being by exploring the physical, mental, emotional, social, spiritual and cognitive benefits.

We evolved with nature. It has had a profound effect on our health and well-being over the millennia, and while it can often seem more challenging to find the time to get outside, we still feel drawn to it to restore, relax and heal.

The benefits of spending time in nature include elevating mood, reducing your risk of heart disease, alleviating some of the symptoms of anxiety and depression, strengthening the immune system, and stimulating better cognition and creativity. Scientific evidence supports the inclusion of all these for better health and to lessen the burden of chronic disease.

If you've been seeking an antidote to the hustle and stress, to restore calm and recalibrate, then look no further. You can think of nature as mental floss, ridding you of all that internal mental clutter that builds up and gives you a nasty headache and brain fog.

If you're currently struggling to find a better balance to overcome the constant demands of work, life and family, increasing your time in nature could:

- help you reclaim clarity in your thinking and bring greater calm to your life
- enable you to reconnect to the bigger picture, to find greater purpose and meaning
- provide you with a clear roadmap to follow in life

- provide the headspace for you to hear yourself think, enhancing your insights and broadening your perspectives
- create a strong sense of belonging, of connection to people and place
- keep you physically and mentally strong
- assist you to live longer and more healthily.

But what is it about spending time in nature that makes you feel good? Why are we drawn outdoors when the going gets tough?

Improving physical well-being

I confess I've never been someone who enjoys going to the gym. I go under sufferance because I know weight training is important for my bone health, and sometimes I need some specific exercises to recover from an injury. But sweating alongside other hot and sweaty people in their Lycra gear in a windowless box with loud music relentlessly pounding my ears is enough to make me want to commit harakiri.

What I do love, though, is walking through my local bushland, spending time down at the beach and simply being outside. This is my happy place, whether alone, with friends or in the company of my two exuberant dogs.

What if you had access to an activity that would lower your blood pressure, keep your heart and lungs healthy and strengthen your immune system while keeping you fit, happy and healthy? What price would you be willing to pay for this?

What if it was already available to you and essentially free?

It's said that success builds momentum. Increase your time interacting with nature by giving yourself permission to do something a wee bit different and try out a new activity, and see whether it's something you might grow to love. This activity might then become part of who you are; there's no sense of it being a chore or wasted time, but rather you welcome the interlude, safe in the knowledge it's doing you good.

As you read the book, I encourage you to pause and reflect on the suggested activities:

- Are these things you used to do and enjoy but just fell out of the habit of doing?
- Are they things you've always wanted to do but somehow never got around to trying?
- Are they things you already enjoy and now have the science to explain why?

You may have friends who are completely hooked on wild swimming, hiking in the wilderness, contributing to community gardens or volunteering to keep the environment free of rubbish. Finding your own special nature hook is easier when it's something you enjoy, look forward to and find fun. That's only going to happen with time and practice.

Maintaining mental health

Environmental psychology is a relatively new interdisciplinary field that examines how our surroundings influence us in every type of environment. While genes play a role in determining health outcomes, we now recognise that our environment plays a bigger role.

While the literature has placed considerable emphasis on the restorative aspects of time in nature for mental well-being, it is also essential to *maintaining* good mental health. A scoping review of the literature in this area found that a whopping 98% of the studies included for review found a 98% improvement in mental health outcomes, along with 83% improvement in physical health and 75% improvement in cognitive health.

Is there any other type of health intervention that comes anywhere close to these findings?

With 10% of the global population living with a diagnosed mental health disorder, the time to start utilising nature-based interventions was yesterday.

If you are someone who has had to deal with a health issue, especially a mental health issue in the past, you know it can recur. This is where nature-based interventions can work their magic, restoring health and well-being and helping you stay well.

Attending to social and spiritual well-being

The impact of shifting your thoughts, feelings and behaviours towards a gentler focus and greater inner peace takes away the constant tension or friction brought on by fighting the system. Your perspective shifts. You smile more. You're more tolerant, less judgmental, and others remark on how well you look.

Cheaper than Botox (and your friends will still recognise you), nature is your natural advantage for living your best life and showing it to the world. The value of adding more time in nature to your routine is immeasurable.

Stress is everywhere, and it's not going to disappear anytime soon. What matters is recognising if this is keeping you stuck or making you sick. Burnout, mental health issues, loneliness and stress-related illness can play havoc with your health and well-being, which is why being aware of what's happening is the first step towards resolution.

Loneliness is a growing social problem associated with multiple pathologies, including poorer overall physical and mental health, lower well-being, poorer cardiovascular outcomes, depression, anxiety, suicide, poorer cancer outcomes, dementia and premature death. When you're lonely, you may feel you have no one to talk to or who understands you. Lacking meaningful social interactions can make us feel socially isolated.

Social prescriptions have become increasingly recognised as one way of combating loneliness. Starting in the UK, today, Canada and the US have a national park prescription program, and here in Australia, there has been a push for greater social or green prescribing. A systematic review and meta-analysis of nature prescriptions in 2023 revealed that these provide many physical and mental health benefits.

It can feel awkward when you first show up at a community event or join a walking group. You don't know the other people, and you're unsure if it's your 'thing'. Can you get your money back if you don't like it?

Committing to showing up allows you to discover what's right for you. It may take three, four or more visits before you notice you're getting into the activity. If you're coming home feeling bright-eyed and bushy-tailed, that's a good sign! Then, as you continue to reap the rewards of feeling healthier and happier, you won't need any reminders to keep going.

Some things are better fixed with items other than medication. The challenge is making these more accessible to everyone.

Also, while your concept of nature may be something you think of going outside to experience, you can invite nature into your home, work, and learning space. Biophilic design is being used to help us enjoy the environment we're in, even if we can't physically touch nature and have to view it through a window or experience it virtually. This is where indoor plants, pictures of nature, natural ornaments made of stone or wood, wood panelling, wood floors, living walls, furniture designed to evoke natural elements and colours, and big windows to maximise natural light come to play.

The next step

I wrote this book to share what I have learned about the science behind the 'feel-good' factor of being in nature.

You may intuitively know you feel better for spending some time outside, having the freedom to go for a walk in the park – to take time out to just sit and observe the movement of the branches of a tree, or follow the dance of a bee busily collecting pollen – but have you ever asked why this is so?

Do you ever wish you had more time to get outside more, or wonder why we have allowed ourselves to become so constrained by the demands of modern life? What if you could create a way of integrating time in nature into your life to feel happier, healthier and just better overall? What difference would that make to who you are or who you want to be?

Do you ever hear yourself saying, 'I wish I didn't feel so stressed, tired, exasperated and fed up'? Every time you play that same record, you embed that negative loop more deeply into your mind. Just like that darn pink elephant, you don't want to think about it, but it keeps popping up again and again and again.

It's time to turn the record over. If you wish things were different, it's time to take action and stop focusing on what you don't want. Instead, ask yourself, 'What do I want?' and focus on that. This strengthens your desire to change your daily routine to bring about the outcome you want – because if you want to change to happen, you've got to really, really, really want it.

If your three-year-old wants something badly, you'll know about it. Why? Because they will keep telling you, often quite loudly, especially when you're somewhere like the supermarket, and they know that throwing a three-year-old hissy fit is more likely to get them what they want than if they stay silent.

Your power for change lies in the strength of your desire, so channel your inner three-year-old and demand what you want.

While researching to understand more about why spending time in nature not only feels good but is good for us, I was especially inspired by Henry.

Henry was fed up. He was over the modern way of work being the be-all and end-all. He felt people were being crushed under the servitude of work and had little chance to enjoy what life had to offer. He wanted to escape his existence of exertion and drudgery that he felt was devoid of meaning and wisdom.

He opted for a tree-change. Henry decided to spend two years living in a small house in the woods near Walden Pond in Massachusetts, focusing on cultivating simplicity and sustainable living. He found nature offered him an immersive experience, many life lessons and an antidote to solitude.

The year was 1845.

We are seeing a resurgence, 180 years later, in interest in and research into what sustains better health and well-being. This is especially relevant now that most of us live in urban environments. Time in nature is not just a nice-to-have – it is essential.

Like Henry David Thoreau, I have learnt many lessons to overcome the stress of modern life and become better equipped to deal with our daily challenges. Becoming a Lifestyle Medicine Practitioner renewed my passion and enthusiasm to assist in reducing the burden of chronic disease that plagues so many of us, and to reveal what enables each of us as individuals to stay well and happy.

Rachel is a lawyer who once told me that whenever a client or colleague asks her a tricky question she finds difficult to resolve, she takes herself off for a swim in the ocean. She laughed as she shared how diving into the water and immersing herself in the briny deep has an almost instant calming effect. She feels relaxed, and as she floats on the waves, her mind processes all those things she's been focused on. More often than not, by the time she gets back onto the beach, she has come up with an answer.

When you have the physical space and time to spend in a natural environment, your body and mind relax, and your psychology shifts. This leads to better health, insights, problem resolution and acceptance.

I'm extremely grateful to those who contributed their thoughts and experiences to this book on how nature has supported, nurtured and healed them. People like Phylicia T:

> Nature has supported me all throughout my life, most notably in the peaks and valleys, in the joys and sorrows, and in states of managing loss, grief, and anxiety in addition to remaining hopeful and inspired, particularly during life's hard patches. I've experienced the tragic loss of multiple family members, childhood abuse (by a family friend), years of infertility, and later a premature birth followed by a miraculous story of my son's survival and a journey of faith, love, and thriving after difficulty. Through allowing my mind and body to be in free-flow, soft fascination with all of nature's natural beauty – from the leaves on trees to the textures of grass, to the morning dew on flower petals, to admiring the vivid, graceful, and unique sunrises and sunsets while practicing deep breathing and sensory connection exercises – I've been able to continuously reduce my levels of stress and anxiety, and fuel greater clarity, self-awareness, and creativity throughout my life, excelling in school and career despite traumatic life experiences.

If you, like Phylicia, are aware of what nature can provide but haven't been able to access the solutions yet, let me take you on a journey in this book to what can help. In the following chapters, I explore some of the physiological and psychological benefits time in nature provides, the science of what is currently known and understood and, importantly, how you can manifest this for yourself.

In each chapter, I suggest you take a moment to ask:

- How does this relate to me in my current situation?
- What is possible for me to do differently?
- How would I feel if I were to do this?
- How much difference would it make to my health, well-being and happiness?

If you're ready to find the answers to these questions, let's dive in.

PART I

RECONNECTING WITH NATURE: WHAT DO YOU NEED TO ATTEND TO?

PART 1

Chapter 1

Sight

'The most beautiful gift of nature is that it gives one pleasure to look around and try to comprehend what we see.'
– Albert Einstein

We rely enormously on our ability to see. It shapes our perception of the world and helps us make sense of it, and it works to keep us safe so we can answer questions like 'What is that?' and 'Where did I put my glasses?' It also shapes our language.

Being able to see has been an enormous evolutionary advantage. It plays a vital role in how we think, remember and track movement. It enables us to distinguish light from dark, sets our circadian rhythm so we know when to be awake or asleep, and provides us with a glorious palette of colour, shapes and texture.

However, the high level of stress associated with modern life and how we operate has affected our visual health, creating tunnel vision, Zoom fatigue, loss of perspective, eye strain and the missing of social and nonverbal cues.

Myopia

When I was in primary school, my mother was called in to speak to my teacher one day and asked, 'Mrs Brockis, were you aware your daughter can't read the blackboard?' My teacher had noticed that I could only read what was written on the board if I sat right at the front of the classroom.

I was horribly short-sighted.

Short sight, or myopia, is a progressive refractive error typically developing in childhood. It often occurs because the eyeball is too long, meaning the focal point is too short, leading to blurry long vision but normal close vision.

The level of myopia is measured in units called dioptres (D):

- Mild myopia is −1 to −1.5 D
- Moderate myopia is −1.5 to −6 D
- High myopia is −6 D or more.

I had −11 D. With a 20-times-higher risk of a retinal detachment compared to someone without myopia or with mild to moderate myopia, bungy jumping is definitely a no-no for me.

Yes, I was blind as the proverbial bat, but unfortunately I also lacked echolocation to help me navigate. Trips to the loo at night meant feeling my way along walls until I hopefully ended up in the toilet and not a wardrobe. At a distance, I could never read the number of the bus I needed to catch to get home, but I had excellent vision for doing things like threading needles. It's a pity I didn't choose a career in microscopic surgery; I could have excelled.

My level of short-sightedness resigned me to wearing a delightful assortment of glasses, with lenses as thick as milk bottle tops and a clear frame topped by either a red or pale blue crescent of colour that Dame Edna Everidge would have delighted in.

I am not alone. Globally, it's estimated that 28% of the world's population is short-sighted. And it's a growing problem. In the United States, half of young adults and 40% of the general population are affected. In developed South-East Asian countries, 80 to 90% of children are myopic. The WHO predicts that 50% of the world's population will be short-sighted by 2050 – that's over 4 billion people!

My maternal grandfather was also extremely short-sighted, so I assumed I had inherited this from him. Thanks, Granddad. However, while genetics do play a role, the dramatic increase in myopia worldwide points to environmental factors.

How screen time makes it worse

The widespread use of television, which began in the 1960s, led to a shift in how children and adults spent their leisure time. Since then, interacting with a screen has become a major factor in our lives, whether it's a television, computer, laptop, smartphone or tablet. Getting your kids off their video games and mobile phones has replaced the problem of them being late home for dinner after playing outside with their friends.

In addition, the COVID-19 pandemic that resulted in home quarantine and online schooling is believed to have contributed to an increased risk of myopia progression in children.

Is concern about screen time warranted? Research would suggest yes. Children under three exposed to screens have a higher risk of becoming short-sighted. More than three hours of screen time a day is associated with a four-times-increased risk of developing myopia compared to one hour, and the risk is particularly impactful for children aged six or seven.

The Australian Government Department of Health and the American Academy of Paediatrics recommend that children spend no more than two hours on a screen outside of school. Yet a report in 2022 showed that children aged eight to twelve years now spend an average of five-and-a-half hours on screen media daily.

What can be done?

How time in nature protects vision

The obvious solution, the simplest and the one shown to work, is to get our kids outside to play. Increasing time outside for play by one hour a week has a protective effect, slowing down a child's deterioration of vision due to myopia.

It comes down to how much natural sunlight comes into your eyes. Natural light is far brighter than any indoor lighting, even on an overcast day. When sunlight contacts the retina, it stimulates dopamine release into the eye. This is thought to help prevent the eye from elongating and reduce myopia risk. Australian studies have shown spending 13 hours a week, or two hours a day, on outside play can reduce children's risk of developing myopia by up to 34%.

It's about the level of lux. When outside, natural light levels are between 11 and 43 times higher than indoor light: 11,000 to 18,000 lux compared to 1000 if you're sitting by a window, while interior environments may be as low as 25 to 50 lux, which is when we put in additional lighting. Sitting under a tree wearing sunglasses will significantly protect children against myopia development.

Sadly, for existing myopes such as myself, time outside doesn't prevent progression.

Screen fatigue

If your work requires you to stay in front of a computer screen for many hours a day, you've probably experienced eye strain. Whether you're peering at a computer screen or smartphone, our 'near work' means our eyes get so used to accommodating close-distance tasks that when you look elsewhere, it takes your eyes a moment or two to adjust. Holding visual focus enhances mental focus, but it is tiring and is different from how our eyes were designed to operate all day long.

Prolonged screen time means we blink less. Usually, you'll blink around 17 times a minute. Focusing on screens can cause that to drop to five to seven times, and that blinking is less complete. This leads to dry eyes, an issue that is compounded by exposure to air conditioning or heating.

How much time do you spend in front of a screen each day? The average worldwide is seven hours a day. Yet, we typically only spend 30 minutes outside.

Once more, nature provides simple solutions. You can improve your visual range simply by getting outside for a few minutes, preferably longer, to stretch your extraocular muscles. Distance vision lowers stress, which feels good, right? You may notice you're more relaxed and less tense. Stress causes your pupils to constrict as part of the fight, flight or freeze response. Lower stress allows your pupillary muscles to relax. Making your visual stretch routine a regular habit makes it easier to focus when required.

Depending on how you work, aim to chunk your focused work into blocks of up to 90 minutes (or whatever is practical for you) and then take a nature break for 15 to 20 minutes. This follows the ultradian rhythm, your naturally occurring body clock regulating energy. Taking a nature break restores your cognition and attention ready for the next chunk of focused work.

Get out in natural light to allow your eyes to relax while you enjoy a visual feast of colours, light and shade. Looking at greenery provides greater soft fascination – your brain enters the default mode, which requires far less effort and helps you relax. Natural green vegetation also helps filter out harmful UV rays and reduces glare. It makes you more creative and puts you in a better mood. Bonus!

When out and about, I often find myself drawn to looking up at the trees around me, watching the branches sway in the wind, listening to the rustling leaves and scouting for the birds I can hear twittering. Looking at a treescape has been shown to reduce stress, and the greater the tree density, the more beneficial the effect.

Blue and green, the predominant colours in nature, improve emotional well-being and lower psychological stress. These colours have lower wavelengths, meaning your eyes don't need to adjust. They are calming and promote relaxation.

Don't forget your hat and sunglasses for adequate UV protection when outdoors. The best ones wrap around your eyes to protect your peripheral vision.

If you can't get away, something simple you can do is to follow the 20-20-20 rule: look away from your screen every 20 minutes and focus on something that is 20 feet away (6 metres) for at least 20 seconds. The joy of having windows is that these provide the perfect way to achieve this, with the bonus that having a green outlook is particularly soothing for your eyes and brain. This also reduces dry eye issues as your blinking rate increases. When you return to your screen, keep it at arm's length and with the font size easy to read to reduce eyestrain.

Bringing nature to you

Scientists have been trying to understand what it is about nature that allows our stress to dissipate. It's believed to be due to fractals.

A fractal is a never-ending pattern that repeats at different scales. Examples include the nautilus shell, tree branches, snowflakes, Romanesco broccoli, coral reefs, ferns, rivers, clouds and coastlines.

In mathematics, the Fibonacci sequence is a series of numbers in which each is the sum of the preceding two numbers. This results in a curve appearing the same at every scale.

Fractals, as found in nature, soothe the brain. They have also inspired human art and design.

Robert Taylor is a physics, psychology and art professor at the University of Oregon. He has long been fascinated by fractals, having first encountered some of the work of the artist Jackson Pollock – whose paintings are now recognised as fractals – at age ten. Taylor believes that fractals are nature's way of being efficient, especially in delivering nutrients. If you look carefully at a leaf, you'll see it has a central vein with many smaller veins branching off it, which means every part of the leaf is nourished. In the same way, the human lung, with multiple branches ever decreasing in size and ending in 300 million tiny alveoli, enables a great amount of oxygen to be absorbed and transferred to the bloodstream. The surface area of the human lung covers an area equivalent to 70 to 85 square metres; that's efficiency in action.

Our visual system has evolved to recognise fractals at a conscious and subconscious level. Research suggests we develop a preference for fractal patterns by age three, indicating that these patterns are significant to us from an early age, triggering automatic responses that lead us to feel calm and relaxed.

It takes the brain a mere 50 milliseconds to recognise a fractal pattern. Compare this to the sluggish 200 milliseconds it takes for it to differentiate friend from foe.

In one of Taylor's most influential studies, he observed what happens in the brain when you walk down a street. Using EEG and MRI scans, he could show an automatic physiological calming effect from nature's fractals, whether actual or virtual, with stress and mental fatigue levels reduced by 60%, which wasn't shown by walking down a city street. He concluded that your brain prefers natural settings, which have fractals, compared to city streets, which typically do not.

Taylor's work continues to bridge the gap between science and human-based design. He uses what he terms 'bioinspiration' to learn from nature and then apply a science-informed human focus to design and architecture.

With stress a major global health concern, aesthetic design is not just lovely to look at; it's vital to human health and well-being. But in many cities, this has yet to be achieved.

Perth, Australia, was known in the 1960s and 1970s for its brown-brick Brutalist public buildings. The word 'brutalism' is derived from the French term *béton brut*, meaning 'raw concrete'. As its name suggests, this style is heavy and imposing, lacks natural light (Brutalist buildings are often windowless) and, in my opinion, is downright ugly. These buildings are functional but lack soul. Having previously worked in a windowless room in a medical practice, I can attest to how depressing that is.

However, biophilic design is now increasingly being used, with interior designers, architects and landscape architects working together to create attractive and stress-reducing environments.

Dr Andrew Leech is a Western Australian GP and pioneer in transforming healthcare. He set up The Garden Family Medical Clinic because, in his own words:

A garden provides a sense of tranquillity and peace. When we go outside into fresh air, surrounded by plants and the sounds of birds or the wind brushing against us, it is a sensory experience that nothing else can replicate. In general practice we see a lot of illness, but what is also important is prevention. We would far more like to prevent disease than have to deal with the consequences of disease. Not all disease is preventable; however, we can all do things to mitigate the onset of illness, boost our immune system and become more resilient. The body needs time to slow down, find space and establish a sense of peace, even if just for a moment. The garden is a place that we can find this.

This biophilic design is to help our patients feel like they are not walking into a medical clinic. I tried to minimise the clinical aspects of a traditional medical centre of a TV, *Women's Day* magazines and old, stained carpets and chairs!

Instead, we have a warm and welcoming reception area and a canopy of leaves held from the roof. The sun streams in from our central tropical garden. Scents of white tea and ginger are infused through our air conditioning. We have soft, calm music playing and comfortable, clean seating, and we replaced the carpet with wood-like vinyl. Every GP room has natural light with large windows, many looking out onto the garden so patients can continue to feel connected to this space. Patients are purposefully seated looking out through the frosted glass when seeing their GP; quite often plants will wave in the wind and brush up against the glass with ferns and bamboo peaking up above the frosting protecting our rooms from the sun. The outlook is peaceful, and I am proud that we have created a safe, inviting space within healthcare.

Simple biophilic elements can be added to a variety of environments in this way, including schools and office buildings, as an easy way of enhancing well-being while reducing stress. Rooms with large windows, living walls, planter boxes, green imagery are far more attractive and soothing to work in.

Taylor is now investigating how to incorporate more fractal elements into indoor furnishings such as carpets, flooring, blinds and solar panels, because as he says, 'We can derive so many benefits from the stress-reducing quality of nature and measurably increase people's well-being by reintroducing nature to design and architecture.'

Add more indoor plants to your home and office. Invite nature in to provide a quiet respite for your eyes by allowing your gaze to shift to the foliage or flowers on your desk or in your indoor environment. You can add fractals to your own environment by:

- hanging some images of nature on your wall
- framing your favourite fractal image and keeping it on your desk
- changing the screensaver on your phone or computer to a natural image
- adding a small succulent or potted plant to your working space, kitchen and living areas
- collecting some seashells and keeping them in a small bowl nearby.

Which fractal patterns are you most drawn to?

Improving eye health through nutrition

Nature can also help our eyes by providing foods rich in nutrients that improve eye health. This is about getting enough antioxidants from your diet, specifically from foods with high levels of vitamins A, C and E:

- Vitamin A contributes to keeping your cornea healthy and assists the rods and cones at the back of your eye to function normally. Dry eye and night blindness from insufficient vitamin A can be prevented by including dairy products, sweet potatoes, fish and dark, leafy vegetables to your diet.
- Vitamin C is found in the vitreous gel between the lens and retina. It absorbs and maintains low levels of oxygen in the vitreous and protects the eye from developing cataracts. Citrus fruits, red capsicum and broccoli are good sources of vitamin C.
- Vitamin E is found in nuts, seeds and vegetable oils, and helps protect the retina's lining.

Zinc works with vitamin A to protect the eye from harmful UV rays. It's found in beef, pork, oysters, chickpeas, beans, cashew nuts, peanuts and yogurt. Eggs contain zinc and help the body absorb lutein and zeaxanthin from the yolk, which also protect the macula region of the eye.

Omega-3 also helps prevent age-related macular degeneration. It is found in oily cold-water fish such as salmon, mackerel and sardines, as well as flaxseed, chia seed, walnuts and canola oil.

In a nutshell

- The heavy screen use of our modern lives increases our risk of myopia developing in childhood. Time outside protects us against myopia development by exposing us to natural sunlight.

- Heavy screen use also leads to screen fatigue. It's important to give your eyes a break from screens by getting outside each day, and thus improving your visual range.
- Looking at fractals, which are everywhere in nature, has been shown to reduce stress. If you can't get out into nature as much as you'd like, you can lower your stress levels by bringing nature inside.
- Eye health can also be improved through nutrition, especially foods with high levels of vitamin A, C and E such as fruit, vegetables, seeds and nuts.

How can you schedule five more minutes a day outside to look at the natural greenery around you and enjoy the natural beauty of the trees, bushes and flowers, or spend time close to water?

Chapter 2

Hearing

'Be silent in your mind, silent in your senses, and also silent in your body. Then, when all these are silent, don't do anything. In that state, truth will reveal itself to you. It will appear in front of you and ask, "What do you want?"' – Kabir

'No other sound can match the healing power of the sounds of nature.' – Michael Bassey Johnson

'Good grief! Not today of ALL days!'

My desk is vibrating from the sound of the compactor working on a block several houses down. The noise of the windows wobbling in their frames makes it impossible to think, let alone get on with my work.

I struggle to quell the desire to shout at the contractors, demanding they 'cease and desist'. I know they are only doing their job.

But I want to do mine.

We evolved to use our senses to gather information and understand our world. While vision may be the sense we rely on the most, our ability to hear and distinguish sounds allows us to detect the subtle changes in a person's tone of voice or to distinguish the different instruments played in an orchestra.

Hearing is the ability to receive auditory information as sound waves that the brain translates into the meaning associated with them. Our ability to connect to and make sense of the world is vital. But the world has become increasingly noisy, resulting in noise pollution that is just as harmful to your health and well-being as other forms of pollution. It's not just the sound of jackhammers, leaf blowers, cars backfiring, or music blasting at high volume that keeps your brain in a constant state of potential threat; it's also the low-level ambient noise of a fan, photocopier, fridge or dishwasher.

No wonder it gets harder to relax or switch off.

Noise

Noise is unwanted sound. It has a physical and psychological component.

The word 'noise' is derived from the Latin *nausea* meaning queasiness or pain, and excess noise is certainly unpleasant to the sufferer. Florence Nightingale, wise woman that she was, is credited with saying, 'Unnecessary noise is the most cruel absence of care that can be afflicted on sick or well'.

In an open-plan office or café, with so much aural sensory input, it can be hard to think, let alone follow a conversation.

When you're at a train station straining to decipher the incomprehensible messages over the speaker system, the poor acoustics not only add to your stress, but you could also get on the wrong train.

If you've ever tried to sleep in a hospital, you'll have noticed there's a lot of unnecessary noise – and you're there trying to get some rest to recover!

Noise is a stressor. There's a reason why we block our ears as we walk past noisy jackhammers, drills, chainsaws and car alarms. It's unpleasant and exhausting, and it makes it harder to think or be heard if you're having a conversation. Too much stress adds to the body's inflammatory load.

Annoying or damaging?

Scientist Mathias Basner reminds us that every time we leave a concert with our ears ringing, we have likely caused some permanent damage to our hearing. One concert maybe less so, but with repeated exposure in this way, the effects are cumulative.

It's not just ageing rockers who go deaf. Workers exposed to noise pollution in work environments of 85 decibels or more (think industrial drills, lawnmowers and blenders) risk deafness and stress-related health problems, including high blood pressure, increased risk of heart disease, sleep disturbance and premature death.

We're advised to keep sounds around us to 70 decibels or below, but without a decibel meter, how would you know? The noise of two people having a conversation is 60 to 70 decibels (although I have friends who I'm sure exceed that).

Noise keeps us awake. It also disturbs the quality of our sleep, causing us to be more restless, wake more frequently and increase our heart rate while diminishing our ability to obtain deep restorative sleep. One night of noise exposure causes your body to produce higher levels of the stress hormones adrenaline and cortisol, leading to stiffening of blood vessels. Over time, this increases your risk of developing hypertension and having a heart attack or stroke. You may well also be very cranky.

Basner tells us that lowering our environmental noise by a mere 5 decibels could save the USA $3.9 billion each year by not having to treat cardiovascular disease.

In 2011, the WHO reported that environmental risks accounted for 25% of the chronic burden of disease, calling noise pollution not only an environmental nuisance but also a threat to public health, with one in three people annoyed by noise during the day and one in five experiencing disturbed sleep.

Noise pollution is now being taken more seriously worldwide because of the recognised detrimental effects on health and circadian rhythms. For example, in 2018, the WHO identified that more than 100 million people were exposed to harmful environmental noise levels, resulting in published noise pollution guidelines in Europe. In 2022, a United Nations report listed noise pollution as a top environmental and health threat. After examining the current scientific evidence, a recent report by the House of Lords Science and Technology Committee in the UK noted how green social prescribing of exposure to natural light and sounds enhances a positive psychological impact.

Research into the mechanisms by which noise pollution harms health is continuing to come up with better ways to regulate it. It's a step in the right direction.

Noise makes it hard to learn

Not only do noisy environments cause stress, they also impair memory, reduce attention and lower learning ability.

One US housing survey found that residents of low-income neighbourhoods were more than twice as likely as others to report bothersome neighbourhood noise levels. Children raised in such environments often have a high level of neural noise in their brains, meaning that their auditory neurons are active even when the external world is quiet. The result is a noisy brain that processes sound less distinctly than it otherwise might. Because of this, children with noisy brains have a harder time learning to read. If you're struggling to make sense of what you can hear, it impacts literacy skills.

Dr Arline Bronzaft is an environmental psychologist who is passionate about the impact of environmental variables on human behaviour. When she heard parents complaining that their children's school, situated alongside an elevated train track, was making it harder for the students to learn, she decided to investigate. Her research found that students studying on the noisier side of the school lagged behind their peers studying on the quieter side of the school. The variability between the two classes was a three- to eleven-month difference by sixth grade. Her findings led to noise abatement strategies, including materials used in the classroom itself, and the New York Transit Authority installing rubber padding on the railway tracks, reducing the noise to six to eight decibels.

The result? The reading scores of the two groups equalised.

The problem of learned deafness

As a child, my family lived on a busy main road. We never heard the traffic, but my friends staying for sleepovers would complain bitterly about how they didn't sleep a wink because of the constant roar of cars and lorries passing by. When we went to quiet rural places on holiday, we couldn't sleep because it was too quiet!

When you're surrounded by noise for much of your day, you stop consciously hearing it, but your subconscious still does. You may have experienced this when you turn off the stovetop fan after cooking – that welcome reprieve is such a relief, yet you hadn't even noticed how noisy it was while it was on. This poses a big danger. Overexposure to background noise interferes with your ability to distinguish meaningful sounds. Being in a noisy place means it's harder to bring your attention to where it's needed because your brain has to decide which noise is most important for your safety. That's tiring.

While you get used to the sounds of traffic, the aircraft flying overhead, the hum, whirrs, bangs and shouts of people and machinery, your brain still interprets them as potential threats, causing you to accumulate stress.

Neurobiologist Nina Kraus, author of *Sound Mind: How our brain constructs a meaningful sonic world*, reminds us that low-level ambient noise is harmful. This includes noise from air conditioners, fans, photocopiers, coffee machines and stovetop fans. The way she sees it, the more we become accustomed to noise, the noisier the world will continue to become, which is bad for us and our brain health.

Do you use headphones and earbuds when out and about? Many of us do, but Kurt Fristrup, a senior US National Park Service scientist, believes this puts us at risk of learned deafness. He and his team have been monitoring noise levels in 90 national parks across the USA and comparing them to urban areas. Worryingly, their findings predict:

> Noise pollution is increasing faster than the US population and is expected to double over the next 30 years ... There is a real danger, both of loss of auditory acuity, where we are exposed to noise for so long that we stop listening, but also a loss of listening habits, where we lose the ability to engage with the environment the way we were designed to.

In other words, if you're missing out on those more natural sounds because of environmental noise or using headphones, finding the peace needed to recover from stressful events becomes harder. Worse still, we stop listening out for them.

Natural sounds – think trickling water, the patter of rain on the roof, the ribbets of frogs, and birdsong – are stress-reducing and calming. If you're missing out on those more natural sounds because of environmental noise or wearing headphones to listen to podcasts, audiobooks or music, it becomes harder for your brain to recover from stressful events.

Natural soundscapes – using sound as therapy

Do you ever yearn for peace and quiet, for a place that provides you an escape hatch to a quieter mind? The solution is to get outside into a natural soundscape more often to lower cortisol and stress levels, alleviate anxiety and improve overall mental well-being. Birdsong, water and wind are the three types of natural sound that have been shown to significantly impact human health and well-being.

Research suggests we prefer natural sound because it's restorative, alleviates stress and aids attention recovery. Other benefits include improved cognitive performance and positive impacts on our emotional state, reducing anger, annoyance and anxiety and alleviating pain. Your individual experience obviously plays a role. If you've only ever known urban life, you might find rural noises quite disturbing!

The National Trust in the UK found that listening to woodland sounds for one minute increases feelings of relaxation by 30% and lowers anxiety. Sixty seconds of natural sounds to feel better? Sign me up immediately, please.

Where will you go for your one-minute interlude of natural sound?

The benefits of birdsong

My husband and I were hiking on the South Island of New Zealand, immersed in the natural beauty of a beech forest in the mountains. Hearing the roar of a river far beneath us told us we were on the right track.

My cousin and his wife, visiting from the UK, had joined us for the day's walk to see the Rob Roy Glacier. It's one of our favourite New Zealand walks, and we were delighted to show them the scenery on a beautiful alpine day. Intermittently, Caroline, an avid birdwatcher, would stop and raise her binoculars, bewitched by the sound of a bird she could hear.

Caroline's frequent pauses on the path made us realise that despite our familiarity with the walk and the pleasure it always provided, we relied more on what we could see than hear. How could we have walked this magnificent trail so often and been deaf to the sound of so many birds?

Because many birds are small, fast and well-camouflaged, it can be hard to see them, which is why tuning in to listen can be so rewarding. Since that day, my husband and I have become better at listening to birdsong when outdoors. We're better at listening to people, too.

Paul and Caroline recounted to me their own story of an experience with birdsong:

> One evening, we drove to a nearby rural nature reserve where several nightingales were reported to be establishing territories through singing. We left the deserted car park and started to walk around a lake in almost complete darkness. With virtually no vision, all sounds were magnified: the background drone of distant traffic, an occasional passing vehicle or plane, and the splashes and alarm calls of water birds. When we were halfway around the lake, we heard a nightingale singing a complex, creative song in the distance.
>
> Then, in another direction, a second, followed by a third across the lake. The surrounding sounds were beautiful and

immersive, but not close. It was a strange but wonderful sensory experience, quite different from a daytime walk.

As we completed the circuit, another nightingale started singing in a tree close to our car. It was so near the sound was almost too loud for our unaccustomed ears. The nightingale sang powerfully, changing its song and experimenting with countless new riffs, trills and variations. We sat on the ground and leaned against a tree, enjoying the intense musical experience. This final, personal concert lasted half an hour at the time but many years in our memories.

Birds don't sing for our pleasure. They sing to attract a mate, or to communicate with each other, such as to sound a warning: be careful, there are humans about!

Hearing birdsong signals you that you're in a safe place. It's when the singing stops that you wonder what's happening.

Hearing familiar birdsong can evoke powerful memories. The sound of blackbirds instantly takes me back to the English countryside of my childhood, while the sound of the kookaburra tells me I'm in my Australian home.

One of the weirdest studies I've encountered came from the California Polytechnic State University. The researchers played phantom recordings of birdsong at specific points along a hiking trail and then asked the hikers about their level of well-being from taking the hike. What they found was that hikers who heard the phantom birdsong for seven to ten minutes reported a greater sense of well-being than those who didn't, and the more species the hikers believed they heard, the better they felt, suggesting that the presence of biodiversity also positively impacts us. Interestingly, no one thought they weren't listening to the real thing, either.

Listening to natural sounds quietens the brain and enhances the parasympathetic nervous system. You're more relaxed, less stressed and better able to cope. Your mind is in a more balanced state, allowing it to make better decisions and think more clearly.

Mental health issues can affect anyone, and nature offers many ways to help, including listening to birdsong. The bestselling book *Bird Therapy* is the compelling story of how Joe Harkness credits birdwatching for saving his life when dealing with depression, anxiety and obsessive-compulsive disorder.

According to Julian Treasure, author of *Sound Business*, birdsong is a useful sound therapy for those of us experiencing noise pollution because it:

- reduces stress
- promotes positivity
- increases productivity
- improves observational skills
- helps you maintain the state of 'body relaxed, mind alert'.

How does it work?

How does listening to natural sounds give us better health, lower stress and less annoyance? This is about understanding your physiology.

In a natural environment, you are more outward-focused. This activates the parasympathetic nervous system, which is restful. In a place of artificial or human-generated noise, however, we are more inward-focused and experience more stress. When you are experiencing anxiety, depression or PTSD, the sympathetic part of your nervous system, the fight, flight or freeze response, is activated.

By immersing yourself regularly in nature, you can use nature and its soundscape to inoculate yourself against environmental stress, allowing you to cope better and build your natural resilience to stress.

Why not give your brain a mental break by listening to natural sounds to refresh and restore your capacity to be relaxed, creative and happy?

The benefits of silence

While certain sounds can be beneficial, they are still additional sounds that we're training ourselves to accept. Sometimes, silence is preferable.

There's a place in the Hoh Rainforest at Olympic National Park in the USA where, if you look carefully, you'll find a small red stone symbolically placed on a log by author and sound specialist Gordon Hempton. The significance of the stone is that it marks the quietest place in the USA.

Gordon needs to come to Western Australia. He'll need to bring as many red stones as he can carry, because this state is blessed with multiple silent sites where there are no intrusions by human-made sounds.

The Quiet Parks International initiative is Hempton's attempt to preserve silent spaces around the world. It's a non-profit dedicated to protecting quiet for the benefit of all life and respecting the quiet of nature.

I've always loved libraries – so many books, so much knowledge and inspiration sitting on the shelves. Best of all, so much quiet, other than the hum of all that cerebral activity as people read. Being brought up to work or study in silence makes it difficult for me to think when music is playing. I can't focus and often end up with a headache.

A two-minute silent interlude between music clips is more relaxing for the brain than listening to soothing music itself; the contrast to the music intensifies the silence's effect on lowering blood pressure.

Other studies have revealed that the brains of mice who were subjected to silence for two hours a day generated new neurons in the hippocampus, the brain area associated with memory, learning and emotional responses.

If you want to do well in an exam, studying in a library or quiet area may benefit you, even if you're not a mouse. Actively listening to silence enriches your capacity to think. In our noisy world, this discipline may be the solution to restore and recalibrate your mind.

In a nutshell

- While sight is our dominant sense, our ability to hear is essential to keep us safe, enable us to understand what others are telling us and interpret what different sounds may signify, even when we can't see what or who is producing them.
- Noise is not only annoying, it can also be bad for our health. It can damage our hearing, disrupt our sleep, impair our learning and even increase our risk of cardiovascular disease.
- We can also develop 'learned deafness', whereby our conscious mind filters out persistent sounds, but our subconscious mind continues to accumulate stress as a result of this noise.
- Natural soundscapes can help to reduce stress by activating our restful parasympathetic nervous system. In particular, seek out birdsong, trickling water, the sound of wind, and quiet places.

What is your favourite soundscape, and how can you listen to it more often?

Chapter 3

Smell and taste

'In every walk in nature, one receives far more than he seeks.'
— John Muir

You smell better than you think.

This is not a comment about your personal hygiene. Rather, I am refuting the commonly held idea that unless you are a trained perfumier, humans are poor at smelling. Not true.

Your sense of smell depends on a small patch of specialised olfactory sensory neurons in your nose that connect directly to your brain, specifically the amygdala, where you process emotion, and the hippocampus, which is involved in learning and forming memory. While we may not be able to match the olfactory prowess of a bloodhound or trained sniffer dog, we can distinguish more than one trillion scents. The point is that we often don't pay attention to our ability to smell or apply it in everyday life.

But just like sniffer dogs, we can get better with training. A 2017 paper found that by getting down to ground level, you can learn to track a trail of chocolate aroma across a field effectively. Think how good that will look on your CV.

Every smell comprises hundreds of thousands of individual odours. Your morning cup of coffee has over 800 different odour molecules, while those in the know can distinguish wines by their multiple odours, from grapefruit to sweaty socks. If you're like me, you read the blowsy labels and attempt to convince yourself you can taste these too.

But the beauty of our unappreciated ability to smell is the health and well-being attributes it provides, as well as triggering memories, impacting your mood and enriching your experience of the world around you. This was brought into focus during the COVID-19 pandemic, when many people experienced anosmia (not being able to smell), which was shown to impair quality of life and emotional well-being.

Introducing phytoncides

If you've ever visited the Blue Mountains in New South Wales, you'll have noticed the blue haze hanging above the trees. Eucalyptus oils combine with dust particles to create the bluish fog, which you can smell.

All plants produce phytoncides, volatile organic compounds including terpenes and essential oils that have anti-microbial, antibacterial and antifungal properties and help plants communicate with each other. For example, if insects or plant-eating animals attack a tree, it can release more phytoncides to warn other trees of the danger. These other trees then start producing more phytoncides themselves to ward off potential attackers. Evergreen trees, including cedar, spruce, conifer, pine and oak trees, have been shown to produce especially high levels of phytoncides.

This is relevant because breathing in phytoncides has been shown by research conducted by Dr Qing Li and Dr Yoshifumi Miyazaki to:

- increase the number of natural killer cells in the body, improving the immune response
- produce an anti-inflammatory effect
- reduce cortisol levels and stress
- reduce blood pressure levels
- lower autonomic nervous system activity so you feel more relaxed and restored
- enhance sleep
- lower blood sugar levels.

Because phytoncide concentration is very variable, being affected by temperature, the type of forest and the season, there's more to forest therapy than phytoncides alone.

When my mother died in 2023, I travelled back to the UK to attend her funeral. During my stay, I went on several walks close to my parents' home. On one of those walks, while taking in the smells of clover and recently cut grass, I experienced a deep, visceral connection to that place, brought on by the memory of time spent on similar walks with my parents, which evoked in me a sense of gratitude and happiness.

Smells that evoke relaxation and lower stress and cortisol levels appear to contribute to our overall health and well-being, especially when there is a strong link to memory. Different memories from different landscapes, whether rural or urban, allow the tailoring of nature-based interventions that are culturally appropriate.

Reducing stress-related disorders with smellscapes

Sensory or healing gardens have been used to assist those recovering from stress-related mental health disorders, trauma and psychological distress.

Stephen Kellert has written extensively about incorporating gardens into architecture and design to reflect the strong connection between humans and nature. Workplaces, too, are realising the benefit of keeping people well by providing access to a sensory garden. Spending 30 minutes a week in this space for a month has been shown to lower stress, enhance well-being and improve productivity – not a bad return on investment for better workplace health and well-being.

Certain specific smells, including lavender, chamomile and bergamot, enhance mood, promote relaxation and reduce stress and anxiety. Planting aromatic herbs and plants near seating areas has been shown to influence brain activity and cognitive function.

We purchase perfumes and eaux de toilette to make ourselves more attractive to others, choosing scents that we like. Floral scents such as rose, lavender, gardenia and orange blossom are very popular. However, research into why natural smells assist well-being has been thin on the ground.

Nature scents can enhance the perception of feeling connected to nature, reconnecting more with the inner self and feeling calm and happy. Pleasant smells in nature enhance physical and psychological well-being by:

- enhancing stress reduction
- evoking pleasant memories

- providing fascination and joy
- building nature connectedness
- evoking pleasant emotions.

Grow a scented garden. Pelargoniums, or scented geraniums, have been a perennial favourite of gardeners since Victorian times. Your choice of scented flowers and shrubs will be determined by personal preference and geographical location. Think lilac, hyacinth, jasmine, gardenias, daphne, boronia, roses, lavender, sweet peas and magnolia. I have a cestrum nocturnum, or lady of the night, in my backyard. It might not be the most beautiful shrub, but its nocturnal fragrance when the tubular white flowers bloom is spectacular.

Does the smell of happiness grow on trees?

The UK is blessed with a lot of woodland, and this type of environment is reportedly the most visited type of green space after urban parks, paths and bridleways. In 2021 an estimate of the mental health cost benefit of spending time in woodlands was put at £185 million (AU$355 million) annually.

One study conducted in the UK sought to distinguish the different levels of well-being associated with specific smells in two different woodland locations over four distinct seasons. Sherwood Forest, of Robin Hood fame, is predominantly oak, while Clumber Park is a mixture of deciduous and coniferous plantation woodland. In each season, participants were invited to visit both sites and think of it like a scavenger hunt to notice the natural attributes of each. They were then divided into focus groups of ten and asked 'What was your impression of this woodland?' as well as what they liked or disliked about each.

Pleasant smells, or the absence of unpleasant smells, were found to impact multiple well-being domains:

- Physical – they felt more relaxed, comforted, refreshed and renewed.
- Emotional – 'joy' and 'happy' were commonly used words.
- Spiritual – they felt calm, peaceful and a greater connection.
- Cognitive – they felt heightened awareness and like they had more headspace.
- General – they felt better and had a greater sense of well-being.

Can you smell the rain?

Some people say they can smell when a storm is coming. Can you?

During a heatwave, with days of intense heat and sleepless nights, it's not unusual to hope a good-sized thunderstorm will come along and clear the air with a downpour of cleansing rain. As the clouds build, you may notice a metallic or clean smell. This is ozone, the name of which is derived from the Greek word *ozein*, which means 'to smell'.

When lightning strikes, atmospheric nitrogen and oxygen are split into separate particles, some of which combine with nitric oxide, creating ozone. Ozone normally occurs in the atmosphere, but you can start to smell it from the downward storm drafts. This is the first smell of rain we can detect.

However, the smell of a good downpour is more than ozone alone. The dank, pungent and wonderful aroma of wet earth is called petrichor, which has three components. Geosmin, from Greek *geo* (earth) and *osme* (smell), is produced by actinomycete bacteria in the soil when they produce spores. Rain assists in the release of geosmin into the air. The third component is oils produced by plants to slow down seed germination when conditions for plant growth are less than ideal; these accumulate in the soil and rocks, which, when rain comes, combine with the geosmin and ozone to provide the complete smell of rain.

After rain, my dogs go nuts, their noses super excited by all the new smells released. Even as poorer-smelling humans, we can still detect a waft of geosmin at a really low concentration of 100 parts per trillion. Other creatures, including flies and camels, are also very sensitive to it, possibly as a means to help them know if there is a water source nearby.

Rain can be a powerful stimulant of memories. For me, it conjures memories of digging potatoes out of the veggie patch at my parents' farm.

Odours for sleep and relaxation

Ancient Egyptians used myrrh to increase sleep quality and decrease fear. My Granny always had sachets of lavender under her pillow to help her sleep. Citrus fragrances have been shown to enhance mood and sleep quality in postmenopausal women.

Hotels and resorts have been hacking smells to create memorable scents encouraging you to rebook. Some even produce unique scented candles for you to buy to take home and relive your memories. Can you remember the scent of your last holiday hotel? Hopefully it was a pleasant smell and not the scent of the drains that left a lasting impression.

Studies have shown that odours modify neural processes during sleep, impacting dreams and sleep quality. One study took a group of adults aged between 60 and 85 and assigned them to receive one of seven diffused essential oils – rose, orange, eucalyptus, lemon, peppermint, rosemary or lavender – for two hours each night. The control group had a substance with minimal smell. Assessments conducted at the beginning and end of the trial assessed brain function – working memory, planning, attention switching and sense of smell – and showed a 226% improvement in auditory verbal learning and improved language function.

Reed diffusers have become increasingly popular. Maybe better sleep and brain function are other good reasons to use them besides the pleasant smell. When inhaled, scent molecules travel directly from the olfactory nerve fibres in your nose to the brain, impacting the area known as the amygdala.

Other research has shown that essential lavender oil can promote subjective and objective sleep quality in healthy individuals.

Using essential oils derived from plants is a popular way of reducing anxiety, easing headaches and improving sleep. Lavender can be used to enhance sleep, lemongrass as an insect repellent, and eucalyptus oil as an expectorant and decongestant.

Other than through diffusers, essential oils are sometimes used as a topical application as when having a massage. Because some of these can cause allergic reaction, it's important to always apply them in diluted form first until you've worked out which aromas you like the best and find most effective for symptomatic relief.

The taste of well-being

'The whole of nature, as has been said, is a conjugation of the verb to eat, in the active and passive.' – William Ralph Inge

'Food reveals our connection with the Earth. Each bite contains the life of the sun and the earth ... We can see and taste the whole universe in a piece of bread! Contemplating our food for a few seconds before eating, and eating in mindfulness, can bring us much happiness.' – Thích Nhất Hạnh

We taste and smell simultaneously, because the same airway connects the nose and mouth. That's why when you have a bad cold and blocked-up nose, everything tastes like cardboard. According to Dr Alan Hirsch of the wonderfully named Smell & Taste Treatment and Research Foundation in Chicago, 90% of what we taste is smell.

We taste using our tongue's tastebuds. Have a look in the mirror. When you stick your tongue out, you'll notice lots of bumps called papillae. Your tastebuds are nestled around the sides of the papillae, looking a bit like segments of an orange. These contain the sensory cells used to help you taste.

You may have been taught that your tastebuds allow you to recognise the difference between sweet, salty, sour, bitter and umami (savoury). That is correct, but your ability to recognise many other individual tastes only arises when combined with smell.

During my surgical internship, I worked alongside a medical colleague who told me she had anosmia (an inability to smell), which meant she only ate because she had to, not because the food gave her any pleasure. I always thought that rather sad, though she said it didn't worry her because she had never known anything different.

While you might not strongly associate your sense of taste with nature, remember our food comes from plants, or from animals that have eaten the plants. Developing your awareness of natural foods and their array of flavours is a fabulous way to enjoy a real taste of what nature provides.

Mindful eating

It was late in the day, and we had just returned to our one-bedroom Airbnb located in a vineyard just outside the medieval town of Erice in Sicily, high on the top of the hill. We had bought crusty fresh bread, basil, olive oil, locally produced mozzarella, and tomatoes for a light supper. Sitting outside eating our meal as the sun set, we exclaimed that the tomatoes were the best we had ever eaten.

Taste is far more than flavour; it's a multisensory experience accompanied by emotion and memories. I've never forgotten the taste of those tomatoes.

One of the mindfulness exercises I teach is mindful eating. Traditionally, this is done with a raisin, but a piece of fruit, a vegetable, or chocolate with a soft centre works equally well.

Start by looking at the raisin. Hold it gently in your fingers to explore what this remarkable fruit looks like, the colours you notice, and its texture. Then, smell it. What do you notice? Is it a pleasant smell? Does it make your mouth water at the prospect of eating it?

Next, pop it in your mouth. Roll the raisin around your mouth; resist the temptation to bite, chew or swallow, and allow all the flavours to bombard your tastebuds.

Finally, it's time to take that first bite as you allow your teeth to penetrate the raisin, continuing to taste as you chew and then swallow.

Mindful eating is useful not just to stop you from eating too fast; it adds to the multisensory experience and savouring. The saliva in your mouth starts the digestive process, connecting you to the hormonal signals your body uses to tell you when you're hungry or full.

Some workplaces provide a designated mindful eating area where employees can sit quietly and enjoy a mindful lunch. Alternatively, taking your lunch outside is an excellent opportunity to slow down and enjoy that mindful break. You might even find it easier to remember what you ate. I know if I've been rushing around and eating on the go, I often don't remember what I had and certainly don't notice what it tasted like.

Nature provides us with food. Honouring the food by paying attention to its preparation, presentation and consumption is a beautiful way to strengthen a positive relationship with our food sources.

Using taste in nature

Next time you're going for a walk in the Australian bush, why not enjoy a mug of hot billy tea? (But if tea is not your thing, it's always a good idea to have water available.) You can use black 'billy' tea, or if you prefer, add one or two washed eucalyptus or lemon myrtle leaves. Wait until the water boils, and then allow the tea to steep for a few minutes. Tradition suggests swinging the billy a couple of times to infuse the water. I don't do this as I'm too worried I'll scald myself. Strain and enjoy.

Native peppermint, basil or lemon verbena leaves can also be used, as can nettles (pick wearing gloves!) and flowers such as camomile. If you prefer other teas, why not take a thermos of black, green or your favourite brew? I use a Jetboil® as it's fast, efficient and very light. I also always take my own supply of water plus a filter (and sterilising tablets) in case I need extra water from a stream.

To keep yourself safe when discovering fruits and berries in the wild, especially if you're not a trained botanist, here are some basic rules to abide by:

- If you don't know what the fruit, berry or fungus is, don't pick it or eat it!
- If you're confident that what you've found is indeed a blackberry, take it home and wash it in case the blackberry

patch has been sprayed with chemicals such as herbicides or pesticides! Avoid eating wild plants growing near farms or roads, and of course, don't steal from someone's garden; otherwise, Mr McGregor will come looking for you, even if your name isn't Peter Rabbit.

- Find out more by going on a nature walk with a trained ranger, buying a book about plants and berries, or taking photos to help you identify things later.
- Adopt a mindful approach to taste.

And if you're going to have a cup of billy tea, you'll need some damper to go with it.

I first saw damper being made when visiting a remote Aboriginal camp in the Kimberley. A couple of older women were sitting on the ground around a fire with some hot coals, mixing flour, salt, butter and water to create a sticky dough. The dough was then kneaded, shaped into flattened rounds, and cooked in the ashes. They insisted I should try some. It was delicious!

Cooking over an open fire is an art form of its own. There is something about sitting around a campfire, toasting your toes (not literally!) and stirring the food in the camp oven – a big, sturdy iron pot with a heavy lid – until it's ready. Pot roast, anyone? My husband and I have had chilli beans, curries, fish, steak and chicken, and jacket potatoes, sweet potatoes or corn cobs baked in silver foil. We've even had fruit crumble and custard. Our appetite always seems bigger when we're camping, and everything tastes great, even when it's a little on the charred side.

If open-fire cooking seems too daunting, many public green spaces provide communal BBQs and grills, perfect for roasting and grilling your food. Or, take your pre-prepared picnic of your favourite foods to share.

Taking in your surroundings while enjoying a drink, snack or picnic is a great way to savour nature. Have you got your picnic rug handy? Then hand out the plates and the food and enjoy.

Grow your own well-being garden

A shared meal, especially when made with homegrown or locally sourced produce, creates memories and strengthens relational bonds. From picking, harvesting, washing and preparing, the shared commitment boosts oxytocin and endorphins.

Growing and cooking our own food is a human pastime that dates back thousands of years. I derive great pleasure from growing and harvesting my own herbs, fruits and vegetables. I get very excited when I see the orange and lime blossoms forming on my citrus trees and the baby tomatoes starting to turn red, and I inspect the fruit frequently as it grows.

The global pandemic saw a rush of people buying plants for their gardens. Nurseries sold out of seedlings overnight as many wannabe gardeners set up their new vegetable patch or herb garden.

Even if you don't have access to a garden or balcony, you can grow a pot of fresh herbs such as basil and thyme on a sunny windowsill. I'm convinced it elevates our culinary experience to a new level! Or is that just in my head?

Here are some suggestions for herbs to grow on your windowsill:

- **Parsley.** Parsley is such a great herb. It tastes so fresh and can be added to almost everything. (Well, maybe not your morning porridge.) Curly parsley has a milder taste. My favourite is the more robust-flavoured flat-leaved parsley. Do you have a preference?

- **Basil.** Will you grow sweet, Thai or holy basil? Whichever variety you choose, harvesting the leaves and adding them to soups, pasta dishes and salads will make you look like a master chef.
- **Chives.** A potato salad is not complete until you've added some delicious snipped chives. Yum.

I've tried to grow coriander without success, but my husband is particularly proud of his chillies.

Encouraging children to participate in growing their own vegetables is also a great way to motivate them to eat them.

In a nutshell

- Our sense of smell is underappreciated and can have a significant impact on our well-being.
- All plants produce phytoncides, which have anti-microbial, antibacterial and antifungal properties. Phytoncides can deliver many health benefits, including reducing inflammation, blood pressure and cortisol (stress) levels.
- Smellscapes have been shown to be effective in treating stress-related mental health disorders, as well as improving sleep quality.
- Your sense of taste is linked to your sense of smell. You can honour the food nature provides you by engaging in mindful eating, eating in nature or growing your own well-being garden.
- Growing your own produce is enormously rewarding, and there's nothing that beats being able to brag, 'I grew this in my garden!'

Chapter 4
Body

'We do not see nature with our eyes, but with our understanding and hearts.' – William Hazlitt

My paternal grandfather died in his mid-forties from septicaemia following a tooth abscess. His death could have been avoided, but he lived at a time when antibiotics were in their infancy. Penicillin was only discovered in 1928 by Alexander Fleming. In the 1920s, it wasn't unusual for people to die at a younger age from infectious diseases such as tuberculosis, smallpox, influenza, cholera or diphtheria.

Until the arrival of the COVID-19 pandemic, most of the current world population had never had to deal with the fear of deadly infectious disease. The Spanish flu of 1918 to 1920 that killed 50 million people (far more than were killed in World War I) and affected 20% of the world's population has long faded into the history books. Today, we are far more worried about succumbing to cancer or Alzheimer's disease. Is this true for you?

Let me ask you a question: what do cardiovascular disease, type 2 diabetes, kidney failure, inflammatory bowel disease, arthritis, Alzheimer's disease, Parkinson's disease, obesity, anxiety and depression have in common?

They are all forms of chronic disease, and they all share a common root cause – too much low-grade systemic inflammation in the body as a result of exposure to chronically high levels of stress. Yes, chronically high levels of stress damage our physical health as well as our mental health. In fact, chronic disease has been ranked by the WHO as the greatest threat to human health, with chronic inflammatory diseases the most significant cause of death globally.

If this sounds depressing, it's important to remember that 80% of chronic diseases are preventable, meaning you can do something about it. So, if too much stress for too long creates all these problems, how can we mitigate its effect?

I'm so glad you asked, because the premise of this book is to provide you with an array of insights, practical tips and tools to achieve this result. Even better, these are all things you can do for yourself, and they are generally either free or relatively inexpensive, and readily accessible.

Cardiovascular disease

Frank was one of my favourite patients. He was one of those people who, no matter what he was going through, always had a smile on his face, a kind word to say and a terrible joke to share.

He loved life, especially playing golf – the course was his happy space. He was out on the course several times weekly, playing 9 or 18 holes, rain or shine.

Frank had severe heart disease. He had been dealt a rotten set of cards when it came to his health, having already survived five heart attacks and several cardiac procedures. He knew his odds of surviving to what he called a 'ripe old age' were slim, but the one thing that he said kept him going was getting out into the fresh air and spending many happy hours on the green.

Whether you're dealing with a broken heart or heart disease, or are feeling a bit low, time in nature not only helps you to feel better but can keep you healthier at the same time.

The biggest killer in the developed world is heart disease. More than just heart attacks, cardiovascular disease includes stroke and peripheral vascular disease. While heart disease, and especially heart attacks, are seen more as a problem for men, heart disease is the leading cause of death in women. The reasons for this are probably best left for another book but include the fact that heart disease may present differently in women, is frequently misdiagnosed, or the woman presents late, meaning she misses out on optimal early treatment. Clinical trials have previously focused exclusively on men, while women's health tended to focus on factors unique to women, including breast cancer, overlooking that a woman's risk of heart disease rises significantly after menopause.

The leading cause of cardiovascular disease and premature death worldwide is hypertension or high blood pressure. The number of people living with diagnosed hypertension globally has doubled since 1990 for a number of reasons, including the fact that we are living at a time of rapid population growth and ageing. It's estimated that currently 1.3 billion adults between the ages of 30 and 79 have hypertension. Hypertension is dubbed the 'silent killer' because it is usually asymptomatic, but if left untreated it can lead to stroke, heart attack, heart failure and kidney disease. That's why it's highly recommended to get your blood pressure checked when you attend a check-up with your health professional.

Blood pressure is measured by two readings. The top reading is the systolic pressure exerted by the heartbeat pushing blood into the arteries. The bottom reading is the diastolic pressure, the heart's resting pressure in between heartbeats. A normal blood pressure reading would look like this:

Systolic pressure: 100–139 mm Hg

Diastolic pressure: 60–89 mm Hg

Your blood pressure is dynamic, changing to suit what you're doing. It's normal for it to be lower when you are sitting or resting quietly than when you are exerting yourself or feeling very anxious.

High blood pressure is commonly idiopathic, which essentially means we don't know why it develops. What we do know, though, is that as we age, our arteries stiffen and become less elastic, meaning our hearts have to work harder to pump the blood around our bodies.

If your blood pressure is consistently higher than recommended, it's time to address the lifestyle factors that may be causing this.

How nature helps

Interest in looking for scientific clues as to why spending time in nature is vital to our health and well-being has steadily grown over the last 50 years. One of the early studies that blew my mind was the 1984 study conducted by Robert Ulrich. He followed the course of patients recovering from gallbladder surgery at a Pennsylvania hospital between 1972 and 1981 to see whether patients assigned to rooms with a green outlook recovered differently to those looking out to a brick wall. While it was only a small study of 46 participants, Ulrich revealed that patients in the rooms with the natural outlook recovered more quickly, were discharged earlier, required less moderate-to-strong post-operative pain medication and did better overall, according to the nurses' reports, than those with an outlook of a brick wall.

In his book *Outlive*, Peter Attia reminds us of some of the contributing factors to poorer health and how focusing on the lifestyle pillars of healthy nutrition, exercise, sleep, socialising and emotional health work to keep us well. He also suggests we should stop focusing on life span and instead look at extending our health span – the length of time we stay healthy without chronic disease.

You may have heard of the Blue Zones, the five areas of the world where many inhabitants live well into their hundreds, remaining healthy and actively engaged in their communities. Dan Buettner is best known for his research into what enables the residents of Okinawa in Japan, Loma Linda in the US, Nicoya in Costa Rica, Ikaria in Greece, and Sardinia to live such long and healthy lives. You won't be surprised to learn that lifestyle factors play an important role. The common threads are that they eat a traditional diet that focuses on local produce that's in season, they are physically active, sleep well, love to socialise and play, and remain highly valued members of their family, being included in all social activities. Being physically active means they also remain active contributors to their local community. The other factor not often mentioned is that they spend a good deal of time outside, working the land, walking, riding horses, cycling or engaging in various outdoor recreational activities.

If you're wondering whether time in nature reduces your potential risk for heart disease, it absolutely does. Two of the largest systematic reviews and metanalyses of the impact of urban and rural green space concluded that time in nature is associated with overall lower mortality and exerts a protective effect against many illnesses, including heart disease.

All physical activity, even slow walking, will help improve cardiovascular fitness. Walking, swimming and other forms of outdoor activity all count regardless of age or fitness level.

Spending 30 minutes a week walking in a green space is sufficient to reduce your risk of developing hypertension, and a minimum of three visits to green space each week is associated with reduced rates of antihypertensive medication. One of the earliest findings from studies looking into the benefits of forest bathing was significantly lower systolic and diastolic blood pressure in the forest environment compared to a non-forest environment.

Your 30-minute walk, on your own or with a buddy or a dog, is not only good for your blood pressure, it will also lower your resting heart rate and improve your lipid profile by lowering LDL cholesterol levels, making your heart more efficient. In addition, living in an area with more green space reduces the prevalence of stroke and makes you less likely to die from heart disease. Bonus!

High blood pressure in children isn't often talked about, but higher blood pressure in childhood is associated with a higher risk of hypertension and heart disease in adulthood. This is why engaging in physical activity outdoors matters at every age.

Touch

'One touch of nature makes the whole world kin.'
– William Shakespeare

'To touch is to give life.' – Michelangelo

A newborn baby uses touch to take in sensory information. In the womb, they are aware of touch from the eighth week of a pregnancy. Touch provides comfort and teaches us about our world, and is vital for improving both our physical and mental well-being. If you've had a rough day, sometimes all you need is a comforting hug.

Touch is a vital part of our sensory system. If you can't feel, you can be at risk of injury. If you receive dental treatment that leaves half of your face feeling numb, you discover just how hard it is to eat or drink. Of course, you also risk burning yourself or dribbling coffee down your shirtfront, which is never a good look.

But are we living at a time of touch deprivation? Tiffany Field from the Touch Research Institute believes both children and adults are touching each other and things less because of the rise of what Jonathan Haidt, author of *The Anxious Generation*, calls 'safetyism' – no-touch policies and the isolation brought about by the use of mobile phones and computers. Tiffany has shown how preterm babies who underwent three 15-minute sessions of touch therapy daily for five to ten days gained 47% more weight than those preterm babies who didn't receive the touch therapy.

Your skin contains various sensory sensors that help you make sense of your world, including temperature, touch, pain, pressure and the position of your joints. We touch to learn about an object, to communicate and to connect. It's how babies explore their environment, conveying everything to their mouths.

Touch is intimate, telling you what's happening in the immediate world around you – unlike sight and sound, which maintain distance. For example, when you pick up a cup of coffee, you can judge if it's hot or cold, the cup's weight and the position of your arm needed to move the cup to your mouth.

We have multiple touch receptors, with the most on the face, fingers, lips, nose and forehead and the fewest on the lower part of our back or the soles of our feet. One type of skin sensor, the Pacinian corpuscles, responds to deep pressure and vibration and is so sensitive that it can react to a skin indentation as small as one micrometre.

We need touch for our well-being. We gain comfort from our mother 'kissing it better' when we fall and scrape our knees. Sensory deprivation causes social pain, as we experienced during the global pandemic, when physical distancing denied us that core need. Children born into sensory-deprived environments fail to thrive, as witnessed by the plight of neglected Romanian orphans in the 1980s.

Telling our children 'Don't touch!' denies them the tools they need to explore. While it makes sense that they don't stick their fingers in a plug socket or the toaster, allowing them to explore nature by climbing trees, creating cubbies out of fallen branches, jumping into muddy puddles, picking daisies and finding natural treasures like coloured shells, different seaweeds or tadpoles in a pond teaches them so much.

Scientists have discovered that when you touch something with your fingers, your eyes stop moving for a fraction of a second. This is believed to help your brain focus and process what you just touched.

Gentle touch helps us cope better with pain. Stroking a dog or immersing yourself in water stimulates nerve fibres in the skin called C tactile afferents, which feels soothing.

Touch impacts the immune system and lowers blood pressure and stress hormones. We employ touch when massaging a sore part of the body. The moderate pressure of a massage stimulates pressure receptors in the skin, increasing what is called 'vagal tone', calming the nervous system and lowering stress. If you've ever wondered why a therapeutic massage feels so good, now you know.

My friend Fiona enjoys a regular massage, and often takes her daughter along with her so they can savour the experience together. On one occasion she booked a 'serenity' massage, where the entrance to the location was lined with leafy Balinese-style gardens and a stone-step pathway to signal this was a relaxing and safe environment. They left afterwards feeling as if they were 'floating on air'.

Touch provides support when someone we see is suffering and helps us feel calm. Touching someone you love or like releases oxytocin, our bonding hormone, which instils trust and strengthens our relationships.

Nature's touch

Whether running your hand through water in a river, brushing your hand across the tops of wheat in a field or brushing away the leaves on a park bench before sitting down, touch is a vital sense for our well-being and contributes to our sense of feeling happy in nature.

There are many ways to indulge your sense of touch outdoors. Lie on the grass. Sit on a rock or against a tree. Walk barefoot. On the beach, feel the sand between your toes; is it coarse or fine? Dangle your feet into a stream; is the water cold? Touch the soil or the leaf litter. Explore the different textures of leaves. Explore the differences in the bark of different trees; why are some rough and others smooth? Pine needles can be sharp when dry and softer when young; what differences do you notice between young growth and mature plants? Notice the rocks and stones around you; are they smooth and rounded or sharp? Why is that? See how many different types of touch you experience when out in nature.

When younger, my kids loved to collect items for a 'touch box'. Their various treasures included feathers, flowers, leaves, stones, shells and seaweed.

Hug a tree. The Tree Hugging World Championships involve speed hugging, dedicated hugging and freestyle, and the competitors take it very seriously. The 2024 Championship was held at Levi, Lapland, in Finland. If you're not interested in competing but would like to get to know a tree better, simply find a tree that you feel drawn to and go hug.

This isn't as bonkers as it sounds. I recently took a small group of individuals on a mindful nature walk and invited them to do exactly this. One participant said she was quite overwhelmed by how good it felt to feel the warmth of the tree's bark against her skin and how it made her feel safe and loved.

At home or in the office, introduce some biophilic elements that invite touch, such as a bowl of smooth pebbles, shells or cones, or living plants with a variety of textured leaves of different sizes and shapes. A living wall not only looks beautiful but invites touch. You can use different textures for wall hangings, carpets and soft furnishings. The use of natural materials such as wood, bamboo, stone, wool or rattan in houses and offices can evoke warmth and comfort. One café I visited had used bark from silver birch trees to create living pictures adjacent to the tables where patrons sat sipping their coffee, providing the illusion of being outside. You can probably come up with lots of your own ideas.

Forester and author Peter Wohlleben suggests playing a game to discover just how good your sense of touch is, to create a mental image of the object being touched:

1. Working in pairs, choose one person to be blindfolded.
2. The other person leads them through a wooded area. You have to trust the leader here!
3. The leader chooses a tree for the blindfolded person to touch in detail, feeling the texture of the bark, the presence of bumps or branches, the leaves, the size of the trunk and the presence of superficial roots or moss.

4. They then return to the starting point, where the blindfolded person is spun around to disorientate them before removing the blindfold.

The question now is, can the person who was blindfolded find the tree that they can now see?

In a nutshell

- Many chronic diseases share a common root cause – too much low-grade systemic inflammation in the body as a result of exposure to chronically high levels of stress.
- The biggest killer in the developed world is heart disease. All physical activity helps improve cardiovascular disease, even slow walking. Findings show that the benefits of physical activity are increased when this activity takes place in a green space.
- Our sense of touch helps us to learn about the world. Indulging our sense of touch in nature is effective for elevating our physical and emotional well-being by lowering stress and blood pressure, which in turn lowers your risk of getting sick and improves your mood.
- Massage reduces stress, eases pain and boosts relaxation. This is because moderate pressure on the skin elicits a parasympathetic (calming) response. Deep tissue massage, anyone?

How can you choose to get more in touch with nature?

Chapter 5

Mind

'Play is the highest form of research.' – Albert Einstein

'To grow up healthy, children need to sit less and play more.'
– World Health Organization

It might not be your current first choice, but did you know you can take a degree in *friluftsliv*?

Friluftsiv, or 'love of the outdoors,' is the Norwegian way of life first described by Henrik Ibsen in 1859. It describes the value of spending time outside to disconnect from daily stress and find greater well-being. Better still, it promotes curiosity, creativity and social development. *Friluftsbarnehager* are Norwegian outdoor kindergartens where the children spend 80% of their time outdoors.

Children intuitively use outdoors play to engage in exploring and learning from their environment. All that running, climbing, jumping, rolling, bending and balancing feels great, reduces stress and anxiety in a jiffy, and boosts endorphins that make us feel so good. It fosters resilience and risk-taking, and nurtures a connection between us and the world around us. It also improves muscular strength and coordination.

Sarah Milligan-Toffler and Richard Louv have written about how exploring, playing and learning in nature improves academic performance more than classroom instruction. And best of all, it's a whole heap of fun. If academic or work performance matter to you, enjoying yourself while learning in a natural environment has been shown to boost attention, imagination, confidence, problem-solving, critical thinking, leadership, teamwork, resilience and cooperation, all of which are essential skills at any age.

As Stuart Brown, author of *Play: How it shapes the brain, opens the imagination and invigorates the soul*, reminds us, 'We are designed by nature to flourish through play'. His work interviewing thousands of people about their childhood has shown how opportunities for unstructured, imaginative play help children grow into happy, well-adjusted adults and promote the continued mental and physical well-being of grown-ups.

Play is repetitive, voluntary and initiated in a relaxed setting. It doesn't need a clear goal. Rules are made up as the play goes along, teaching fairness, turn-taking and better communication. Children's play boosts the release of brain-derived neurotrophic factor (BDNF), which stimulates neural development for emotional and social learning.

The first known forest school was established in Denmark in 1952 by Ella Flautau. She and her neighbour's children began gathering each day in the forest as a sort of unofficial form of day care. Three- and four-year-olds spent time in natural woodland or forested areas, where they were encouraged to explore and learn from their environment. Forest schools have since spread to Europe, the UK, the US, Australia, New Zealand and Asia – and, naturally, the children who attend them are having a lot of fun. As the data and research continue to support the forest school model, the hope is that more open-air classrooms and free outdoor play will reduce the current emphasis on stressful, busy, curricula-stuffed schedules and a high level of screen time.

The academic performance of Finnish children is the envy of the world. The difference? Until a child reaches school age (seven), Finnish day care focuses on creative play and being physically active outside. In school, every class is a maximum of 45 minutes long, and classes are separated by a 15-minute outdoor break for all children and their teachers in all weathers, except when the outside temperature drops below 20 degrees Celsius.

Neuroscience has shown that this is the ideal way to learn, and children are encouraged to develop a love of learning rather than focus on grades.

A Danish study of over 900,000 people found that those who grew up as children with more green space to play in had a lower risk of developing a psychiatric disorder, mood disorder, schizophrenia or substance abuse in later life. Naturally, the best green schoolyards are those designed by and for the school community, where students, teachers, parents and community members can play, learn, explore and grow. Beyond the school playground, there are many ways communities and families can ramp up the time children spend outside. The aim is to meet the minimum recommendation of 60 minutes each day.

'Safetyism' and technology are getting in the way of play

All work and no play makes Jack a dull boy and Jill increasingly anxious. Did your Mum tell you to go outside to play when you were young? Mine too.

Jill was my best friend in primary school. She lived next door to some allotments, where we spent countless hours creating cubbies in the surrounding bushes, playing make-believe and generally having fun. While we were left to our own devices, our parents knew where to find us when it was time for dinner. We would go home somewhat grubby, with mud and grass stains on our knees and clothes, very tired and happy.

We know how important time outside for play is for childhood development and well-being. However, our fears of the what-ifs and unknowns are obstacles to allowing our children to experience the freedom, fun and independence that unstructured and unsupervised play provides, and that we remember enjoying ourselves. Today's children spend 50% less time in unstructured outside activities compared to the 1970s.

It's easy to point the finger at the bad news bombarding our television screens, parental concern about stranger danger and unsafe play equipment. Then, of course, there's our new favourite babysitter: the tablet, smartphone and video games that keep our children inside, safe on the couch and entertained.

The biggest consequence of this is the adverse effect it's having on our children's health and well-being. Insufficient time outside to play and be active is leading to shorter lives for these children compared to their parents and a greater risk of chronic disease, including heart disease, obesity and type 2 diabetes, as well as poorer mental health, with an increased risk of depression in adulthood. As Louise Chawla, Professor Emerita in the Environmental Design Program at the University of Colorado Boulder, reminds us, 'Within a generation, children's lives have largely moved indoors, with the loss of free-ranging exploration of the nearby natural world'.

As parents, our desire for our children to be happy and healthy and do well at school appears universal. Yet, despite all our good intentions, our children's mental and physical health is in decline. Are you worried by the amount of time your children spend inside, relatively motionless? Worldwide, it's estimated that 77.6% of boys and 84.7% of girls are insufficiently active. Outside play is being replaced by increased screen time, which has the knock-on effect of reducing the desire to go outside.

The statistics tell us that an increasing number of children between the ages of 18 months and five years are dealing with separation anxiety disorder, autism spectrum disorder, ADHD, sleep issues or anxiety. Issues observed in those aged between six and 12 years include social anxiety, ADHD, friendship issues, problematic screen use, and educational and learning concerns, while those aged 13 to 18 display the highest increase in depression, social anxiety, general anxiety, suicidality, self-harm and friendship difficulties. One study showed that every extra hour of sedentary behaviour each day increased depressive scores by 10% by the age of 18 years.

Researchers agree that children who spend more time outside are happier, more focused and less anxious than their indoor-orientated peers. Time in nature builds confidence, autonomy, and responsibility, and encourages creativity and imagination.

Going on walks of between one-and-a-half and three hours has been shown to support adolescents' mental well-being and reduce stress and anxiety levels. These walks boost relaxation and peace of mind, foster gratitude and temporarily get away from what's been causing them stress. Even 10 to 20 minutes a day in nature has been shown to reduce stress and psychological distress in 18- to 22-year-olds. However, a bigger drop in cortisol levels comes from being outside for 20 to 30 minutes. More is better! As Anne Frank said, 'Nature brings solace in all troubles'.

Some nature-based educational programs have been specifically designed to assist children having trouble in mainstream education, who are neurodivergent or have mental or physical health issues. One example is the wonderfully named Muddy

Puddle Teacher approach created by Sarah Seaman in the UK in 2018, which follows the three M principles:

- mother nature (and the source of mud)
- mental health
- moving.

The thought of muddy maths makes me think how much better I might have been at learning the subject outdoors. You can find out more at themuddypuddleteacher.co.uk.

In the 1970s and 1980s, outdoor education in the UK school system meant sport: tennis, netball, hockey, football and athletics got us outside and active each week. Once a term, a class excursion to a local natural beauty spot or historical place of significance allowed us to learn about geography, history or biology. The latter were always my favourite; you could keep your hockey. I remember very little from our classroom lessons in school, but the memories of some of the places we visited are etched strongly in my mind and nurtured a lifelong interest in the subjects.

It's not just the kids who benefit from learning outside; teachers have reported they enjoy the outside activities because they see how much more engaged and attentive the children are. In addition, following an outside learning activity, children continue to pay better attention and remember more information.

Calmer, healthier children who are intrinsically motivated to learn are every teacher's dream. One survey reported that outdoor learning and play lowers stress and boosts happiness, engagement, mental health and understanding of the environment.

Outside play for grown-ups matters too

Play alleviates stress and makes us smarter. How? By developing more creative thinking. That's why play for adults is so important for our overall cognitive health. It makes us better prepared for life and work's curveballs, encourages experimentation and safe risk-taking and helps us retain the mental energy needed for creativity and innovation by reducing stress.

The outdoors is the perfect playground in which to relax, have fun, interact with our children and try new activities. Currently, around 30% of Australian adults engage in exercise, sport or an outdoor activity such as walking, running, swimming, sports, water sports, fishing, golf and cycling for one-and-a-half hours a day.

As George Bernard Shaw said, 'We don't stop playing because we grow old; we grow old because we stop playing'. Giving yourself permission to play outside more often is a wonderful way to extend your own skills, foster a greater appreciation for the great outdoors and strengthen social connection with others, whether your family, friends or others you meet along the way. Accessing green or blue space is something we can all aim to do more regularly to assist in lowering stress and stimulating greater insight for problem-solving.

There are now many examples of workplaces introducing biophilic elements either into the workplace itself, with living walls, plants and rooftop gardens, or constructing green space that is easily accessible during work breaks or outside meetings. Taking employees offsite to a natural environment works wonders to build engagement, stimulate new ideas and foster interest in how to improve productivity and performance.

Creativity and innovation are highly sought after at work, but having the headspace to achieve this when weighed down by everything else that must be done can feel impossible. Perhaps you've noticed how you feel much more invigorated after a couple of days away in a natural environment. You feel cognitively sharper, and you're more energised, bright-eyed and bushy-tailed. Not only that, but your mind is also brimming with new ideas and you can't wait to share them.

If only we could experience this more often! Maybe you can by setting the intention to use nature to boost your creativity and well-being more often.

How nature helps us to be more creative

Creativity is the generation of new (and valuable) ideas. It involves identifying a problem and realising potential solutions.

It's time to ditch the idea that creativity is a right-brain function. Neuroscientists have discovered that creativity draws on the whole brain at a conscious and subconscious level and includes our emotions. This may explain why creative people are frequently portrayed as fiercely passionate and enthusiastic about their work.

What if time in nature – in one study this was a four-day hike, totally disconnected from multimedia and technology – could lead to a 50% increase in your ability to think creatively?

The way many of us have been taught to problem-solve is to pay close attention to the issue, analyse it from top to bottom, tune into our previous experiences and work out a logical solution. This is how the executive attention network works. This can work well, but it denies more divergent thinking, where we come up with multiple ideas which may be fanciful, remembered from our past, or original. Time then allows us to percolate and evaluate our thoughts, resulting in either a delightful 'Aha!' or inspiration to further nurture solutions. This is the default or 'imagination' network at play; far from being at rest, this is when our brains are most active. You may have noticed, too, how insight often comes at a time when you least expect it, like when you're in the shower or walking the dog. That distraction works brilliantly to disengage you from thoughts that may be stuck fast on a solution that doesn't work.

A natural setting away from your usual environment allows you to rest and enjoy some soft fascination with your new setting and a little mind-wandering. Sitting to watch the clouds moving across the sky or the trees bending in the wind allows your mind to roam to places it normally doesn't have the time and space to get to. When feeling stuck or mentally fatigued, going for a walk in nature, or even just looking out of a window onto a green space, serves to restore attention and stimulate a greater sense of calm.

Mental fatigue occurs because when we are at work or driving, we are being bombarded by 11 million bits of sensory information per second. Our brain has to filter this to derive the 15 to 20 bits it determines are most relevant and worthy of our attention at the time. It is little wonder, then, that we are so cognitively fatigued and stressed by the end of our busy day. Without sufficient mental breaks or cognitive pauses, we drive ourselves harder and faster to the point of exhaustion.

Nature helps by allowing you to experience unnoticed things that stimulate your brain without exhausting you and lower stress, helping you find greater mental clarity. You can think of spending time outside as your opportunity to reset and allow your overtaxed prefrontal cortex, which has been involved in all that cognitive heavy lifting, to recover.

Getting into that space of flow where you're totally immersed in your thoughts, where everything comes together beautifully and you're delighted in your mental progress, is further helped by enjoying the process. When you're feeling inspired and motivated, it's so much easier to do the necessary work.

Joining a creative group can work wonders. That's why creative retreats can work so well. You're in a space where others are simultaneously involved in bringing ideas to life.

However, sometimes being alone will work better. There's nothing I enjoy more than time alone with my own thoughts. Solitude brings me peace and serenity to reflect, find meaning and join the dots of my thinking. When absorbed in the beauty of the natural world around me, I'm curious as to what makes it so, and this keeps my mind open to greater possibility.

Artists have long been inspired by nature, such as painters Claude Monet, Vincent van Gogh and Georgia O'Keeffe, poets William Wordsworth, John Keats and Robert Frost, sculptors Henry Moore, Andy Goldsworthy and David Nash, and architects Frank Lloyd Wright, Antoni Gaudí and Fariborz Sahba. However, you don't have to be a recognised artist to enjoy your creative side, and we are all creative, even if your primary school art teacher suggested you weren't.

Engaging in nature more frequently, whether as a deep dive or a brief encounter, can fuel your creative side. It's up to us to schedule the intention, perhaps starting with 10 to 15 minutes a day in a natural place you enjoy being in that feels sufficiently detached from your usual environment, is immersive (that is, you're surrounded by nature) and provides enough natural variety to trigger your interest in exploring the area.

David Lynch is a famous filmmaker whose book *Catching the Big Fish* reveals his own ideas around creating ideas. He writes, 'Ideas are like fish. If you want to catch little fish, you can stay in the shallow water. But if you want to catch the big fish, you've got to go deeper'. The implication is that the more wild the natural environment, the greater the impact on creativity, but work with what is available, even if it's an urban, green setting.

Fundamentally, children and grown-ups flourish when allowed to play outside. For children, play that is unstructured and nature-based provides essential developmental skills to set them up to grow into healthy, well-adjusted adults.

Playing in a natural environment with your family teaches them that you value time outside for fun activities. Letting your children see you let your hair down, have a laugh and relax while enjoying outside activities encourages important life skills and fosters their own love for the natural environment.

Outside experiences create strong memories. Do you remember being taught by a parent how to swim, sail or fish? Did you explore rock pools together or go on nature trails?

Encourage your children to create their own art using sticks, stones and leaves. You can also create your own.

An Australian friend of mine has young grandchildren who live in Canada. When they heard Grandma was going on holiday to a beach, they requested that she build a picture on the sand using seaweed, shells and pebbles, and share a photo of it.

I think Grandma had as much fun creating her seaside art as the kids did in seeing the result.

In a nutshell

- Spending time outside not only lowers stress and improves well-being, it also boosts attention, imagination, confidence, problem-solving, critical thinking, leadership, teamwork, resilience and cooperation.
- For children, outside play fosters curiosity, creativity and social development, as well as resilience and risk-taking.
- Children are spending more time inside nowadays, and this has been linked with social and mental health problems.
- Time in nature is also important for adults in improving creative thinking and innovation, important skills for work and study.

Chapter 6

Soul

Taking time out from our busy lives can sometimes feel too hard, even when the reward is inevitably positive. The feeling of always being rushed or not having enough time to complete all our tasks is wearing and a common factor of modern life.

We intend to be on time and to remember, but how often do you realise you've missed your physio or hairdressing appointment because you got waylaid by something else that came up? Time has become a precious commodity we'd like more of.

And yet, have you ever noticed what happens to your sense of time when you're on a pleasant walk, pottering around the garden or enjoying the warmth of the afternoon sun while relaxing in a park? When that level of frantic activity dissipates, you enjoy that time rather than fighting its passing too quickly. In a natural environment, time feels longer somehow. How good does that feel?

Walking in nature for an hour has been shown to reduce activity in the amygdala, the part of the brain involved in processing stress. Also, research has shown how individuals who moved to a greener urban area reported an immediate improvement in their mental health that lasted three years, and those who moved to a less green urban environment experienced a drop in their mental health upon moving, which recovered to its base level over time.

The mental health benefits of time in nature are profound, including lower stress, reduced anxiety, increased life satisfaction, and fulfilling psychological needs.

Chronic stress

We all experience varying levels of stress in our lives. That's normal. What's not normal is feeling over-busy, overstretched, overwhelmed and constantly exhausted.

Some stress is normal, because it helps us respond to the stressor or threat, whether a job interview that's coming up, meeting your partner's parents for the first time or being asked to perform on stage. It's good to have that tingle of excitement, anticipation and hope that all will go well. It prepares you to do your best. It's chronic stress that's the problem, the relentless pressure to always be striving for more – more status, more promotion, more money and more material goods.

Our levels of chronic stress continue to rise. Depression is the leading cause of disability globally, anxiety is causing our younger generations in particular a huge amount of distress and loss of function, and burnout at work now appears to be almost expected.

Burnout, described by the WHO as an 'occupational' syndrome, comprises extreme physical and mental exhaustion, negativity and cynicism, and a drop in performance due to exposure to chronic stress that has not been successfully managed and is going from bad to worse. It is a complex, multifaceted syndrome commonly accompanied by symptoms of anxiety, depression or panic. While certain personalities may be at higher risk – namely the perfectionist, high-achieving, dedicated individuals who care deeply about their work and the people they serve – the issue lies squarely at the feet of those organisations that tolerate or even condone overwork, toxic behaviours and unreasonable workloads.

Burnout is pervasive and affects many individuals. When severe, it can result in the affected person taking a significant amount of time off work – the current average is 17 weeks, and the average worker's claim cost runs into the tens of thousands of dollars.

Burnout is a symptom of more stress being put onto individuals than they have capacity to deal with. According to Gallup, Australians experience some of the highest work-related stress rates in the world – 81% of the Australian workforce, compared to the global average of 73%. That is not the gold medal to aspire to. Despite the introduction of psychosocial safety legislation to help protect employees, that sense of running on empty is doing us harm and adding to the risk of developing associated mental health conditions such as anxiety or depression.

Yet, burnout and mental health problems can be treated and even prevented using lifestyle medicine principles, including time in nature. This is why 'getting away from it all' helps to provide a sense of freedom and safety.

Using nature to assist with chronic stress and mental mood disorders

One of the biggest shifts in thinking about health has been moving away from the idea of separating physical from mental health. However, this idea is not new; Scottish physician William Buchan wrote in 1769, 'Of all the causes which conspire to render the life of a man short and miserable, none have the greater influence than the want of proper exercise'. We are whole beings, and it's long been recognised that what affects the mind often has implications for the body, and vice versa.

Professor Michael Berk, Director of Deakin University's Institute for Mental and Physical Health and Clinical Translation (IMPACT), says there is a special connection between inflammation and both physical and mental health; as mentioned previously, it's now known that coronary heart disease, Alzheimer's disease, rheumatoid disease, inflammatory bowel disease, bipolar disorder, schizophrenia, anxiety and depression all share this common background.

Lifestyle medicine practitioners already adhere to the idea that if you are suffering from depression, one of the most effective treatments is exercise, especially outdoor exercise, which leads to the increased production of endorphins and serotonin, lowering inflammation and improving mood. Research from the University of South Australia found exercise 1.5 times more effective than counselling or medication in the management of depression, anxiety and psychological distress, and suggested physical activity should be a mainstay approach. Walking, jogging, strength training, yoga, tai chi and qi gong are all effective interventions. Best of all, exercise can be used as a preventative measure.

All types of physical activity are beneficial, though those requiring more time and more intense physical activity work best. However, don't underestimate the power of a gentle walk or even sitting quietly in nature. Stepping outside, even for a few minutes, has a positive effect on mood and mental well-being. Ten minutes of light exercise positively impacts mood, and 12 weeks of this practice has a long-term impact.

Ten minutes helps, but more is better. Spending between 20 to 90 minutes outside has been shown to be best for elevating mental health. You get the biggest bang for your buck during the first 20 to 30 minutes of being outside; after that the benefits accrue more slowly. And it doesn't matter what time of day it is or where you are, so long as you feel safe.

This is not to suggest that time in nature is the panacea to all mental health challenges or replaces the need for medication or other therapies, or even that everyone derives the same benefit. However, it is a powerful adjunct and can complement the use of medication and cognitive behaviour therapy.

Ecotherapy is a type of formal treatment that involves doing activities outside in nature. Studies have shown this helps alleviate symptoms of stress, anxiety and depression through the combination of physical activity and social contact outdoors. Just looking at a green view rather than concrete buildings for five minutes has been shown to calm the mind through activation of the parasympathetic system, slowing down your heart rate and rate of breathing.

While nature acts as a buffer to our daily stressful events, it also changes our behaviours and promotes better psychological and mental well-being. In urban environments, access to green and blue spaces provide multiple opportunities that promote more physical and social activities.

There are many possible nature-based interventions, including horticulture, wilderness therapy, ecotherapy, nature-based arts and animal-assisted interventions. They can be used by people of all ages, as well as by specific at-risk or vulnerable groups.

New apps are making it easier to include nature into your daily routine. For example, NatureFix allows you to access a series of nature well-being walks in public spaces to boost mood and improve mental health, increase nature connection, decrease stress and support social and environmental actions.

Mind Over Mountains is a UK-based charity founded by Alex Staniforth and Chris Spray in 2020 to help individuals restore and sustain their mental health and well-being in nature. CEO Ian Sansbury explained to me that their aim is to assist in restoring mental health naturally by providing people with time to heal in the form of weekend retreats in beautiful locations such as the Peak District and the Lake District. The retreats include two days of hill-walking, life coaching, mindfulness breaks and meditation under the guidance of a mountain trail leader, a coach and professional counsellors. They also provide one-day hill walks. What makes interventions like this work is having an effective partnership between health professionals, the practitioners who run these programs, and suitable, readily accessible natural assets.

Forest bathing

Tomohide Akiyama, Director General of the Japanese Ministry of Agriculture and Fisheries in the early 1980s, recognised that the Japanese work ethic of long hours and little time off was literally killing people. The term 'karoshi' means 'death from overwork'. Technostress was already being recognised at that time as a significant contributor to levels of workplace anxiety, depression, mental fatigue, insomnia, irritability, heart attacks, stroke and suicide.

Karoshi was initially seen as a problem peculiar to the Japanese, but this is a global issue. The WHO has stated that working more than 55 hours a week is associated with a 35% higher risk of stroke and a 17% higher risk of dying from heart disease compared to working 35 to 40 hours a week. Too much work is a health hazard, recognised as responsible for about one-third of the total estimated work-related burden of disease.

Akiyama believed that spending time in the woods did people good, while distance from nature made people sick. In response to karoshi, he came up with the concept known as *shinrin-yoku*, or 'forest bathing'. Since 2004, the Ministry has also been involved in a series of projects to investigate the therapeutic effects of what has become known as 'forest therapy'.

With 70 per cent of Japan covered in forests and trees, it's relatively easy to access one of the 65 accredited Forest Therapy trails. Having booked your session, you meet up with a medical professional who takes your blood pressure and measures your heart rate variability (an indicator of your heart health) both before and after your two- to three-hour nature immersion, during which you are invited to undertake a series of nature connection activities. Naturally, you can also take yourself for your own forest walk without a guide or medical intervention.

By deliberately slowing down, you start to feel calm and more relaxed. This triggers a number of physiological changes, including lowering your blood pressure, cortisol and blood sugar levels, strengthening your immune system, and alleviating symptoms of anxiety and depression.

Today, *shinrin-yoku* is practised in many countries, including the US, Canada, Chile, Finland, Sweden and South Korea. The UK even has The Forest Bathing Institute which has partnered with the University of Derby to further investigate the physiological benefits of forest bathing. The Institute defines forest bathing as a health-promoting nature-connection practice that aims to enhance well-being, relieve stress and encourage relaxation.

In New Zealand, *rongoā* is a traditional Māori healing system that similarly harmonises the body, mind and spirit.

As immunologist and forest therapy expert Qing Li says, 'There is no medicine you can take that has such a direct influence on your health as a walk in a beautiful forest'.

Loneliness

> *'During my years caring for patients, the most common pathology I saw was not heart disease or diabetes; it was loneliness.'* – Vivek Murthy

The scrappy piece of paper half-submerged under a sea of other information on the common room noticeboard grabbed my attention: 'Room to let. Battersea.' And a phone number.

I called and spoke to a kind-sounding man who turned out to be a registrar in the hospital I was working at. After a short interview to see if I would be a suitable tenant, I had a new place to call home.

Until then, I had been in shared student accommodation. But we were only allowed to stay for 12 months, and the time was up. Now, I was on my own. The house wasn't far from the hospital, so I could cycle to and from work. All seemed good.

However, I missed my friends. We were working on different wards, doing different shifts, which made it hard to meet up. Days off were spent alone in my room. Sometimes, I'd hop on a bus and go to Oxford Street to spend money I didn't have. The less I saw of my friends, the worse I felt. I was with people all day long at work, and in London every street was full of people walking, chatting, shouting and laughing.

I stopped going out socially. I called in sick at work more often with gastro, severe period pain and migraines.

I was horribly lonely.

As Olivia Laing, author of *The Lonely City: Adventures in the art of being alone*, says, 'You can be lonely anywhere, but there is a particular flavour to the loneliness that comes from living in a city, surrounded by millions of people'.

Six months later, another scrappy piece of paper on the noticeboard announced several student-share flats were available in Southwark. Salvation had arrived.

As a committed introvert, I crave solitude. I love spending time alone with my thoughts, preferably in a beautiful place, just to be. But I hate loneliness, the sense of being apart or disconnected from others – like when you find yourself at a party where you don't know anyone, and you're stuck in a corner with a drink while everyone around you is engrossed in their conversations or gyrating to the music with their friends.

Loneliness is the subjective experience of being alone and lacking meaningful connections, which causes distress. In 2023, the WHO declared loneliness a pressing global threat affecting one in four people.

One outcome of the global pandemic has been the worsening of social connection and increase of social isolation. At a time when we have never had a greater ability to connect using our digital gadgets, it seems bizarre that we are experiencing a loneliness epidemic. Dr Michelle Lim, the Chief Scientific Advisor for Ending Loneliness Together, writes that one in three Australians report feeling lonely or very lonely. Around the world, 24% of men and women surveyed report feeling lonely. That's an awful lot of lonely people.

If you've ever felt lonely, you know just how painful it can be. It can destroy your confidence and self-worth, creating a self-perpetuating downward spiral of lost hope and trust.

The irony is that we push others away when we need human connection more than ever. Loneliness should not be ignored because it has a detrimental effect on every aspect of health, both physical and mental. It shortens lives.

It's an issue because humans are hardwired for social connection; we flourish in the company of others because it provides us security and that all-important sense of belonging. Since Aristotle observed that 'man is by nature a social animal', we have recognised that we have an innate need to belong. In his book *Social: Why our brains are wired to connect*, author Matthew D Lieberman reminds us that as hunter-gatherers, we depended on our tribe to survive and procreate. Our brains evolved not merely to think but to plan what we anticipate will happen next from a social context. Our magnificent brain is a social organ.

This is why loneliness is so painful, but we have yet to figure out how to combat it effectively. Managing loneliness is not so hard when it's short-lived, but chronic loneliness creates distress and poorer physical and mental health, and shortens lives. It's been shown to be as bad for your health as smoking 15 cigarettes a day. It is as bad as the combination of obesity and a lack of physical activity or consuming six alcoholic drinks a day. Being lonely is highly detrimental to your health. It is associated with higher rates of depression, heart disease, stroke, cancer and premature death.

Those at greatest risk of loneliness are young adults under the age of 25 and those over 65 years. However, anyone of any age can experience it.

Loneliness is frequently invisible because we're very good at making it so. As with mental health and burnout, there's a stigma around being lonely, which explains why 58% of lonely people say they don't talk to others about their loneliness and 31% say they feel ashamed about the way they feel. It's not something we want to shout about from the rooftops or even admit to our best friend.

Social connection is vital to individual and community health. It fosters academic and career achievements. It creates greater happiness and well-being, which leads to engaging in more prosocial activities and behaviours. Your stress levels lower, and you cope better with life's curveballs. You become more resilient, tolerant and understanding of others.

One of the biggest issues in our busy lives is that despite living close to and working with other people, our long work hours and fatigue make it difficult to meet new people with whom we might become friends. It's harder as adults to meet people when we change jobs, or move interstate or overseas and away from our family and existing circle of friends. In one survey, 47% of respondents said they believed they would feel less lonely if they knew more people.

Why are we experiencing greater loneliness now?

Thomas Astell-Burt, Professor of Cities and Planetary Health and Australian Research Council Future Fellow on nature-based solutions for well-being and loneliness, believes we have created a 'lonelygenic' environment through three factors:

1. the urban effect associated with overcrowding and high population density
2. the modern life of being stuck inside or working from home
3. reduced opportunity for meaningful face-to-face contact – technology can present a false image of reality.

Fundamentally he argues that urban spread has led to a heavy and growing reliance on our cars even for short errands. He blames car traffic for dominating residential roads, which are also clogged by parked vehicles, leading to 'the loss of the people-friendly streets that we once used for regularly gathering, playing and celebrating with neighbours. No wonder we now know so few by name. If the determinants of loneliness are largely environmental, so too must be the solutions. Yet we hear so little about this'.

The more time you spend alone, the higher your risk of loneliness. Once you're spending 75% or more of your time alone, loneliness starts to become difficult to avoid. The bizarre thing about feeling lonely is how it makes you feel that no one else understands what you're going through, yet 25% of people are also feeling lonely in their own unique way.

Loneliness changes your social behaviour and how you react to other people. The resulting 'threat state' means that while you crave belonging, you lack trust and are hostile towards others because you fear further social rejection.

Overcrowding, population density and social isolation have been shown to increase the risk of loneliness by 39% and the risk of death by 45%. However, this can be counterbalanced by as much as 28% if you can see trees or the sky, or hear birdsong, as shown by a study that used an app called Urban Mind. Data was collected from more than 750 people living in urban environments around the world (in the UK, Europe, USA and Australia). Participants were asked simple questions three times a day on loneliness, overcrowding, social isolation and contact with nature; 16,603 assessments were undertaken, which included the questions 'Do you feel welcome among the people around you?' and 'Can you see trees right now?' This assessed the degree of loneliness in the moment, acknowledging that it isn't a constant emotional state.

Assessing the degree of loneliness experienced can predict mental issues such as anxiety and depression, alcoholism, suicidal behaviour and cognitive decline, as well as immune and cardiovascular disease. Feelings of social inclusion were shown to reduce loneliness by 21%, and by an additional 18% if this coincided with time in nature.

Using nature-based interventions to combat loneliness is an obvious but mostly overlooked possibility.

Green prescriptions – how access to nature helps combat loneliness

As a GP, I saw many people I recognised as lonely in my practice. While prescribing time for a cuppa and a chat isn't listed as a Medicare benefits option, many health practitioners today prescribe what are known as 'green prescriptions'.

Green prescriptions provide opportunities to connect with community groups and projects. Spending time with like-minded individuals fosters a sense of belonging and support, and stronger social bonds. It lowers stress and blood pressure levels, and enhances mood, all of which enhance well-being.

Sue Stuart-Smith, psychiatrist, psychotherapist and author of *The Well Gardened Mind*, reminds us of our innate connection with nature, and how our heart rate slows and our blood pressure drops after just three to four minutes of being in a garden.

In community greening programs, local residents are invited to participate in creating and maintaining local green space. Spending time in nature makes us feel better, and joining a group in this way opens up opportunities to make new friends while enjoying the social activity.

Community gardens have a long history in the UK and have been on the rise over the last few years. They are the perfect place to learn and improve your gardening skills, share knowledge and cuttings, and, of course, have plenty of time to chat. City farms, care farms and community gardens are popping up faster than you can say 'zucchini'. The Royal Horticultural Society and the UK charity Social Farms & Gardens state they are on a mission to support more communities to farm, garden and grow together 'from Belfast to Brighton, Skye to Swansea'.

The Golden Hill community garden in Horfield, Bristol, is a wonderful example. The garden is open every Wednesday from 10 a.m. to 4 p.m. and aims to increase the skills and confidence of local people in growing food through volunteering and training.

In Scotland, doctors teamed up with the NHS and The Royal Society for the Protection of Birds to connect patients to nature-based activities.

In Sydney, Australia, the Community Greening program supports over 637 different community gardens that are co-designed and co-built by the community, tailored to their needs and the local climate. Over in Victoria, the Healthy Parks Healthy People initiative has worked to increase engagement from diverse communities across the state through their volunteering programs. In Western Australia, community groups such as the Grounded Women Gardening group in Bunbury combat loneliness by planting fruit, vegetables and flowers together.

New Zealand initiated its Green Prescriptions program in 1998 to encourage more individuals to be active.

In 1999, the USA started its own social prescribing program, Prescription Trails, believing that parks contribute to the community's health. This led to the launch of Parkrx in 2013, with the introduction of a free day pass to state parks upon presentation of a prescription from a health provider. Practitioners are provided with guides, toolkits and case studies to encourage their patients to use their prescriptions.

PaRx is Canada's first national, evidence-based nature prescription program. They also have a virtual nature prescription.

Social or green prescriptions tick all the boxes for physical, mental and social well-being. Green prescriptions are available to those considered vulnerable or at risk, including immigrants, older adults, socially or linguistically isolated populations, and those who may not have had much exposure to time in nature before. But you can always self-refer too!

I've been part of a weekly walking group for several years. Initially, it was a way to catch up with a friend. We would meet early in the morning, agree on our route through some natural bushland and head off for an hour. Now, we are a small group. Having a planned regular walk with friends quickly becomes something you look forward to. Walking, jogging, ocean swimming or cycling – there's something for everyone.

If you're new to an area and have yet to create new social connections, joining a group like parkrun can help. It started as a time trial at Bushy Park in Teddington, London, in 2004; 13 people turned up. Today, parkrun has over 9 million people registered and is held in multiple locations in over 20 countries as a free, volunteer-led 5 km run, jog or walk each Saturday morning at specified locations. It's even endorsed by the Royal College of General Practitioners (RCGP) and the Royal Australian College of General Practitioners (RACGP). It's open to all ages and levels of fitness – 93-year-old John Day has completed 500 parkruns! He says he loves it because it makes him feel a little bit fitter, and he enjoys the run and the scenery, seeing people he knows and meeting new people.

Making quality urban green spaces more accessible to all

Any nature-based interaction, whether fleeting or sustained, has the potential to drive social cohesion and prosocial behaviour. This is especially true for urban green space. Even just exposure to images of green space has been shown to influence an individual's willingness to help others, enhance perspective-taking (because we are drawn out of our tendency towards self-absorption) and increase prosocial behaviours with greater collective engagement.

If you live in an area where 30% of the nearby land comprises parkland, woods and reserves, you have a 26% lower risk of becoming lonely than those with less than 10% of nearby land being green space. This is why taking specific measures to increase green space in our densely populated cities matters to build a stronger sense of community and belonging. If loneliness resulting from increased urban living can be helped by contact with nature, having improved access to urban green and blue spaces is increasingly important.

Australian researchers Thomas Astell-Burt and Xiaoqi Feng have identified several pathways to reduce urban loneliness by creating local networks of green space that provide value to all. For instance, if there are no trees or open green spaces nearby, why not look for planter boxes with seating and sustainable green landscaping?

The RECETAS (Re-imagining Environments for Connection and Engagement: Testing Actions for Social Prescribing in Natural Spaces) project is a wonderful initiative by ISGlobal to carry out a five-year, large-scale research and innovation project involving 13 institutions from 9 countries. It was set up in response to the finding from before the COVID-19 pandemic that 75 million Europeans only meet with family or friends once a month and 30 million frequently feel lonely. The challenge of the project is to analyse, understand and evaluate how nature in the city can promote social interaction, help combat loneliness, and improve the health and mental well-being of urban populations.

Positive solitude

> *'If you learn to really sit with loneliness and embrace it for the gift that it is… an opportunity to get to know you, to learn how strong you really are… you will realise that a little loneliness goes a long way in creating a richer, deeper, more vibrant and colourful you.'* – Mandy Hale, *The Single Woman: Life, love, and a dash of the sea*

Perhaps you've noticed that when you're feeling lonely, spending time in a green space helps reduce stress or symptoms of anxiety and stimulates your desire to be more prosocial. Spending time alone in a green space feels calming.

Positive solitude is when you're happy to spend time with just yourself for company, relishing the lack of interruptions and distractions. Having the space to be and to enjoy nature, whether going for a coastal walk or tramping across some hills, can feel liberating, freeing you up to think, reflect and feel less stressed. It provides the space required for self-reflection and a connection to the wider world, giving a sense of purpose and direction.

It's about finding the happy balance between enough positive solitude and less of the negative, and you are the best person to know what's best for you.

Mindfulness

Mindfulness practice has enjoyed a surge of popularity over the last few years as a way to help us manage our cognitive load. A form of meditation, mindfulness is a cognitive skill learned through practice. It involves quieting the mind by paying attention, on purpose and without judgment, to the present moment. Many cultures have embraced it as a practice to reduce stress, improve mood, restore energy and sharpen focus.

When feeling overwhelmed, anxious or stuck, taking a natural break to practice a brief meditation can help restore calm and inner peace, enhance your observation skills and cultivate a deeper appreciation for the world around you. It allows you to slow down and take yourself off autopilot.

The neuroscience of mindfulness meditation has found it reduces stress by enhancing emotional self-regulation. Lower stress nurtures neuroplasticity, the brain's ability to rewire itself in response to the changing needs of the environment.

It's particularly effective when conducted in nature. A short mindful pause in the multisensory environment provided by nature sharpens all your senses while enhancing awareness of your thoughts and emotions.

While meditation may conjure up an image of a person sitting quietly on the ground with their eyes closed, informal mindfulness meditation happens when you walk silently along a trail or sit in a pleasant spot observing your surroundings. It's an easy way to enhance the positive aspects of spending time in nature.

A mindful pause could involve:

- stopping to observe the bark on a tree
- looking up at the waving branches of the tree canopy overhead
- watching an ant carry its load over a path
- following the stop-start flight of a bird moving from bush to bush.

Belinda is an environmental scientist based in Perth. Her own personal experience of using meditation to manage a difficult event in her life led to her training as a meditation teacher, ultimately combining this practice with being a forest guide. She explained to me what led her to create her own business, Mindful in Nature:

> I found my sanctuary while growing up in the heart of Western Australia's south-west. Among the tranquil wilderness, I sought solace from the chaos of adolescence, forging an unbreakable bond with the natural world that would shape my life's path.
>
> My journey took an unforeseen turn with a single phone call bearing distressing news of a loved one's health. In the years that followed, as I navigated the labyrinth of emotions and responsibilities that came with being a pillar of support, I turned to meditation.
>
> Through the practice of mindfulness, I discovered a profound resilience within myself. I transcended chaos and found serenity amidst life's turbulence.

Driven by my own transformation, I embarked on a path to become a meditation teacher. Yet, it wasn't until I delved deeper into the interweaving realms of meditation and nature that I unearthed a revelation.

Guided by *shinrin-yoku*, deep ecology, and *dadirri* principles, I rediscovered my innate connection with the natural world, recognising it as a wellspring of wisdom and healing. My journey became a testament to the profound synergy between mindfulness, meditation and nature – a synergy I now share with others through immersive experiences and transformative workshops.

Today, my teachings offer a profound reawakening to the interconnectedness of all things and the transformative power of simply being present in the natural world. Participants are invited to observe and immerse themselves in the rhythms of nature, finding renewal, healing and a deep sense of belonging amid life's challenges.

Time in nature enables greater self-compassion. Self-compassion is not always easy. When recovering from trauma, getting out into nature is soothing and helps you to overcome some of your pain and suffering.

Belinda uses a mindfulness technique called RAIN, which was coined by Michele McDonald and made popular by Tara Brach:

- Recognise what's happening
- Allow and accept the experience to be just as it is
- Investigate with interest and care
- Nurture with self-compassion.

Can adopting RAIN in nature help you deal with the trauma in your life?

Nature-based mindfulness enhances physiological, psychological and social well-being. Wild nature is more beneficial than a more cultivated setting, but what you choose depends on what is available and accessible to you. Spending time in any green space will be of benefit.

Whatever form of meditation you choose to practice, start by putting yourself into a calmer and more relaxed state first by taking several slow, deep breaths and feeling your belly rise as you do so.

Here are some ways that you can practise mindfulness in nature:

- **Go for a slow walk.** This is less about the distance covered and more about simply being in nature and observing your surroundings. Where possible, find a quiet path with little human or other interference. Notice your feet as they touch the ground. Some people prefer to walk barefoot; do what feels right to you. Aim to synchronise your breathing with each step, keeping everything slow and calm. Looking at the beauty around you, how does it affect your appreciation for what nature provides?
- **Practise a sit-spot meditation.** Find a favourite spot and sit on a small cushion or mat. Spend a couple of minutes focusing on what is around you. Is there a bee foraging for nectar, a small lizard basking on a warm stone, or an attractive shrub with brightly coloured flowers? What do you notice? What's changing around you? Are the shadows lengthening, is the sun setting, or are the clouds changing shape and form as they pass by?
- **Use an app for outdoor meditation.** Sometimes, listening to a guided meditation allows you to choose the length of your meditation practice. I love to find a quiet spot near the sea

where I can listen to my meditation set against the soothing rhythmical backdrop of the sound of the waves reaching the shore.

Awe

'I would rather have a mind opened by wonder than one closed by belief.' – Gerry Spence

'The moment one gives close attention to anything, even a blade of grass, it becomes a mysterious, awesome, indescribably magnificent world in itself.' – Henry Miller

Whether it's gazing starstruck at the Milky Way against the velvet black backdrop of a night sky, that jaw-dropping moment when you see an extraordinary landscape, or witnessing the intricate perfection of a spider's web silhouetted by dewdrops in the sunlight, these are the moments that take our breath away.

We experience awe in many ways, such as by watching dance, listening to music or visiting extraordinary buildings and nature. These events inspire joy and gratitude and simultaneously reduce the stress and worries we otherwise spend too much time thinking about. Awe conjures up the understanding of our true insignificance, and it feels good.

Professor Dacher Keltner from the University of California, Berkeley defines awe as 'the feeling of being in the presence of something vast that transcends your understanding of the world'. Keltner has described how the collective human experience of awe benefits our health and well-being. It contributes to a greater synchronicity of our nervous system, heartbeat and other people around us.

It's reported that awe promotes greater humility, counteracting our more selfish proclivities of entitlement, arrogance and narcissism. Our friends are more likely to rate us as humble, and we enhance our ability to present a better-balanced view of our strengths and weaknesses.

Awe is also considered adaptive. Awesome new information that piques our curiosity helps us absorb data and change our responses to ensure our survival while continuing to extend our knowledge and understanding of the world around us.

Dopamine is an important neurotransmitter involved in the brain's reward circuitry. When triggered by awe, the mind is opened up to wonder, exploration and a reduction of inflammation. It increases empathy and reduces self-preoccupation.

It's possible to find awe in many places. Journalling your own experiences will give you an idea of how often you feel it. Studies have shown that it's common to experience awe two to three times a week. Awe isn't something that you have to wait for or travel to exotic places to obtain. By doing the things that provide you with meaning, being aware of their impact on your psyche and taking the time to open your mind to what is around you, the magical mystery tour of life will show you awe in myriad places. Just take a moment to pause and see.

Awesome adventures

Some of our biggest adventures occur in the smallest of places, like taking your toddler for a walk down the street and letting them explore the cracks in the pavement, the piles of leaves, the plants growing in brickwork, the bark of the trees and the fallen seed pods. Rarely do we ever take this type of mindful walk to discover what's in our surroundings. It might take half an hour to cover 50 metres, meaning there is a lot to find! Witnessing your child's wonderment is awesome in its own right.

Other forms of awesome adventure could involve challenging yourself to do something a bit out of your comfort zone, like hiking alone, going white-water rafting or cycling part of the Tour de France route. Perhaps you could sign up to join a group visiting an area you've never been to.

The magical benefits of seeking awe manifest in a number of ways:

1. **You're doing something different.** Getting out of the office, changing your routine, slowing down to fully enjoy that cup of coffee in the sunshine, and looking around you to take in everything new takes you out of the constant state of busyness. Watching an insect feeding on nectar, the miracle of a butterfly emerging from its chrysalis or a bird feeding its young takes you out of the ordinariness and makes you witness to the extraordinary. After just ten minutes, your stress levels start to drop. Your mood and focus improve, and your blood pressure and heart rate begin to settle.

2. **It doesn't feel like exercise.** Not everyone loves going to the gym. It's hard work, you get sweaty and, apart from loud music, there's not much to distract you from your bodily discomforts. However, cycling through a local park, walking through wetlands to see the birdlife, kayaking up a gorge or walking a famous route like the Camino de Santiago are all activities that don't necessarily feel like exercise but are. A couple of days away and you'll already feel fitter, happier and less stressed.

3. **It expands your perception of time.** Awe creates a time warp where it feels like you have more time available. This lowers stress, assists decision-making and increases your willingness to volunteer, try other new things and be more satisfied with life. This is because the moment of wonder keeps you in the present moment. Your well-being just went up a notch or three.

4. **You've achieved something!** As captain of your life ship, getting to your destination feels fabulous, especially if the journey was challenging. The more difficult your personal challenge, the greater the sense of satisfaction in your achievement. And those achievements are meaningful. They are now etched firmly in your mind as wonderful memories you can draw upon at any time – along with a few hundred digital snaps to show to your friends. Remember when...?

5. **You discover who you are.** Try this experiment with your friends. (It's OK, they won't come to any harm.) Ask, 'Who are you?' and listen to their response. If they tell you their name and where they live, fine. However, studies have shown that people who experience more awe in their lives are more likely to describe themselves in more universal terms – 'I'm a human living on planet Earth' or 'a member of the human race'. In other words, awe promotes social identity in collectivist terms. It promotes an effect called 'small self'. We feel insignificant and vulnerable in the context of the world around us. When returning from a camping or walking expedition away from other humans, noise and all the accoutrements of modern life, it's normal to have a decreased desire for materialism, you no longer crave up-to-the-minute news, and you are more critical in your thinking about what you're being exposed to or desire to be a part of. And that's pretty awesome in itself.

6. **Awe brings connection.** Feeling connected to place and planet is very calming and grounding. Australian First Nations people experience a strong connection to 'country'. It's their very being. Similarly, our connection to where we are born and our homeland stays with us, even when we may move to live far away from that place. I've lived in Australia

longer than in the UK, where I was born, but even now, revisiting those places associated with my childhood evokes intense feelings of knowing that this is where I'm from, and it makes me happy. Also, spending time in places of natural beauty has been shown to inspire greater generosity and willingness to help others, either through volunteering or helping as the need arises.

Dark skies

There's something very alluring about sitting under a starry sky gazing at the Milky Way.

The Milky Way, so named because Greek legend holds that the goddess Hera sprayed milk across the sky, comprises billions of stars. Our solar system orbits around the Milky Way, taking a mere 230 million years to complete one circuit.

Seeing the night sky in all its glory is important for our sleep patterns and natural circadian rhythms. Even one immersion into dark nature strengthens the immune system, and the benefits last up to four weeks.

We used the night sky to navigate, plan harvests and track time. However, our relationship with darkness changed as we lit up our homes, streets and office buildings.

Unfortunately, we don't get to see the stars as much anymore because of light pollution. Between 2012 and 2016, light pollution (artificial night-light) increased by 2.2%, which may not sound much, but it's estimated that 80% of the global population and more than 99% of US and European residents now live under light-polluted skies. Only 2% of the UK population is estimated to receive a truly dark sky. But did you know 60% of our biodiversity depends on darkness to survive?

In case you were wondering, the darkest place on the planet that we have measured is at the Roque de los Muchachos Observatory on La Palma in the Canary Islands, where artificial light only brightens the night sky by 2%.

Stargazing reminds us of our insignificance in the greater scheme of things. It builds a connection to nature and the world around us. Here are some ideas for how you can access greater awe in darkness:

- Go for a night-time walk. Why not make it part of your evening routine? Go alone or with someone else. Take a torch, preferably a red light, to prevent tripping over or twisting your ankle in a rabbit burrow.
- Plan a full moon walk, night fishing trip or kayak with friends.
- Choose to camp in a natural site with a low risk of contamination from artificial light or sound pollution.
- Turn off the lights in your home and backyard and step outside. What do you notice?
- If you're into photography, why not learn how to take pictures of the night sky?
- Look up your nearest Dark Sky Place at darksky.org.

The first Dark Sky Place was established in 2001 at Flagstaff, Arizona. Since then, over 200 Dark Sky Places and 20 dark sky preserves have been established in 22 countries.

Here in Australia, the River Murray International Dark Sky Reserve northeast of Adelaide is exceptionally dark, measuring around 21.8. Other dark locations include Aoraki / Mount Cook National Park in New Zealand, Brecon Beacons National Park in Wales and Death Valley National Park in California.

Mark Westmoquette, author of *Mindful Thoughts for Stargazers* and *The Mindful Universe*, shares:

> Not many people realise that the night sky is as part of our natural environment as a forest. And the great thing is you don't need to go anywhere to see it – all you need to do is step outside, or even just open the curtains.

In a nutshell

- Chronic stress rates are rising globally. Spending time in a green or blue space has been shown to help.
- Despite humans being hardwired for social connection, loneliness affects one in four people. We're spending more time than ever inside, making it harder to create meaningful connections with people. Ways that nature can help combat loneliness include green prescriptions – especially social prescriptions, such as joining a community garden or walking group – as well as making green spaces more readily available and embracing positive solitude.
- Mindfulness has been found to be effective at reducing stress. Combining mindfulness with time in nature, which has inherent soothing properties, can boost its effectiveness.
- Awe promotes greater humility and counteracts entitlement, arrogance and narcissism. Seeking awe in nature can provide many magical benefits, including boosting your physical activity, improving your mood and self-esteem, and providing opportunities for connection. Dark Sky Places are a great example of where you can find awe in nature.

PART II

NATURE'S MEDICINE

Chapter 7

Air

'Of all the remedies I have used or seen in use, I can find but one thing that I can call remedial for the whole disease... and that is a profuse supply of fresh air.' – Florence Nightingale

'Fresh air is nature's way of reminding us that every breath is a gift.' – Shree Shambav

'Breathing in, I calm body and mind. Breathing out, I smile. Dwelling in the present moment I know this is the only moment.' – Thích Nhất Hạnh

I always look forward to arriving at Queenstown Airport in New Zealand – not just because of the majestic snow-capped mountains we cruise past that feel close enough to touch as we descend towards Lake Wakatipu, but because when we step outside, I can smell the freshness in the air. I take big, deep gulps of that beautiful, crisp, clean air that reinvigorates me and reminds me why I love this place so much.

The cleanest air on the planet is at a place called Kennaook. This pristine environment is one of 25 sites worldwide where scientists collect and analyse air samples to monitor air quality.

It's also known as Cape Grim, named as such by Matthew Flinders because of the dreadful sea and weather conditions he experienced there in 1798. It's beautiful, wild, rugged and remote, and frequently battered by strong westerly winds, the Roaring Forties that travel from Antarctica. Don't stand too close to the cliffs – gusts up to 180 km/h have been recorded.

If you can't get to Kennaook, you'll be pleased to know that Australia has the most cities with fresh air, with six experiencing 365 good air days. That's phenomenal! Good air days are determined by the level of air pollution, where levels of fine particulate matter known as PM2.5 (because they have a diameter of 2.5 micrometres) are low. In case you're wondering, Zurich, Reykjavik and Honolulu are among the cities with the cleanest air.

If you've ever watched sunshine streaming through a window, you will have seen the myriad dust and other particles floating in the air. The air we breathe contains far more than oxygen, carbon dioxide, argon, water vapour and nitrogen; it has its own microbiome, just like our gut. Moreover, atmospheric winds can transport these microorganisms and pollutants for thousands of kilometres.

To see how the air quality where you live compares to the rest of the world, the World Air Quality Index project has a webpage (waqi.info) that shows the real-time air quality at 10,000 different monitoring stations.

The problem of smog

We breathe to live by obtaining oxygen, which makes up 21% of the earth's atmosphere. Breathing is a signal that you are alive, but most of the time we're unaware of it unless we've had to run for the bus, or climb four flights of stairs because the lift isn't working, or are having an asthma attack.

As a childhood asthmatic, I never took breathing for granted. On one occasion, I had an asthma attack while out walking on the North Downs with my dad. He had to carry me back to his surgery (he was a vet) to give me oxygen.

Asthma remains the leading chronic disease in children. It's a chronic inflammatory airway disease that remains a public health challenge. Its rising prevalence, along with allergic rhinitis (hayfever), eczema and chronic obstructive pulmonary disease (COPD), is thought to be due to increasing air pollution, prolonged exposure to aeroallergens, extreme weather events and changes in biodiversity.

A couple of years ago, while in Beijing to speak at a conference, opening the bedroom curtains of my hotel room in the morning revealed a thick brownish haze smothering everything outside, with visibility reduced to just a few hundred metres. 'The air is good today!' said the concierge brightly as I stepped outside. *Really?* I immediately started to cough and felt my eyes stinging and throat burning. Even when I escaped the city to visit part of the Great Wall, I was struck by how far into the countryside the haze lingered. The air quality in Beijing is so poor the pollution regularly exceeds safe levels by tenfold.

Our small population in Australia means air pollution doesn't reach the same level as for those living in megacities like Beijing or Delhi, which have a high population density, congested roads and poorly monitored industries pumping pollutants into the sky. The paradox is that our air pollution is more likely to come from natural events like bushfires rather than industry and traffic.

Air pollution is the world's single most significant environmental cause of preventable disease and premature death. Air pollution in the form of particulate matter is linked to a range of human health conditions, including bronchitis, glaucoma, heart attacks, autism, high blood pressure, cancer, cognitive development problems in children, dementia, heart failure and increased mortality.

We know smoking is bad for us, but the long-term health effects of smog exposure are equally if not more devastating, with the WHO indicating that air pollution causes 6.5 million premature deaths each year. In Australia, air pollution is linked to more than 3200 deaths each year at an estimated cost of $6.2 billion, attributable to premature mortality and reduced life expectancy associated with the increased risk of cardiovascular and respiratory diseases, along with increased rates of hospitalisations, birth defects, impaired cognitive function and use of medications.

Some of the common air pollutants known to impact human health include:

- ground-level ozone (O_3), which is harmful to lung health
- particulate matter, especially PM10 and PM2.5, which creates hazy skies and associated health issues
- nitrogen dioxide (NO_2)
- carbon monoxide (CO)
- sulphur dioxide (SO_2), which irritates the lungs and contributes to acid rain.

Because carbon dioxide (CO_2) naturally occurs in the air, it's not normally considered an air pollutant, but human activity, especially burning fossil fuels, deforestation and land use changes, have contributed to greater concentrations of CO_2 in the atmosphere, making it a greenhouse gas.

We tend to associate air pollution with respiratory disease, but it also significantly contributes to poorer brain and heart health. Globally, air pollution causes around one in five deaths from cardiovascular disease, and it's a particular risk for those with pre-existing heart disease.

Sources of air pollution include:

- exhaust fumes from cars, trucks and other vehicles (particularly those with diesel engines)
- traffic-related pollution, including tyre and brake wear
- bushfires or fires for cooking or warmth
- indoor woodfire heaters
- agricultural activities (farming) and waste burning
- industrial activities such as manufacturing and food production
- second-hand tobacco smoke
- dust, dampness and mould
- chemicals, cleaning products and indoor floor-polishing equipment.

Leaves – our natural air filters

You may be asking, 'OK, how can nature play a positive role here?'

I want to take you back to my school biology classes, where we learned about photosynthesis and transpiration. Performed by plants, algae and certain bacteria, this is one of the most important biochemical processes on the planet, because it provides the oxygen we need to live.

Let's remember, too, that more than half the oxygen we breathe is derived from phytoplankton and seaweed in the oceans. A marine cyanobacterium was producing oxygen 3.5 billion years ago, long before the first land plants evolved from green marine algae 470 million years ago. Prochlorococcus is the most abundant marine photosynthesiser on the planet – it produces a massive 20% of all the oxygen in our atmosphere – and it was only discovered in 1988.

Leaves are green because their cells contain chloroplasts, specialised to absorb sunlight and use carbon dioxide from the atmosphere, water obtained through transpiration from the roots and the sun's energy to produce oxygen and glucose. This process helps to reduce the amount of carbon dioxide in the air. Oxygen is then released into the environment, while the plant or tree uses the glucose for growth.

The US Forest Service has found that a large mature tree can absorb the equivalent of 21 kg of carbon dioxide a year. Putting that into context, this is the same amount of carbon dioxide emitted by an average car driven for 41,000 km.

Stomata are tiny, microscopic pores found mostly on the undersurface of leaves; they are where gaseous exchange takes place. During the day, carbon dioxide is absorbed and oxygen is released, and the reverse occurs at night. The stomata are also responsible for absorbing gaseous pollutants, including sulphur dioxide, nitrogen dioxide, carbon monoxide and ozone, which are broken down once in the leaf.

It's estimated that one large tree can provide a day's oxygen supply for up to four people! Not only that, photosynthesis powers 99% of the earth's ecosystems, enabling us and the rest of the planet to survive.

And there's more. Particulate matter in the air is harmful to human health. Trees and plants help by catching these on their leaves, branches, and trunks. When it next rains, the particulates are washed off onto the soil or stormwater. This process can effectively remove up to 4 tons of airborne pollution per 2.59 sq km, impacting the body's immune response, protecting us against the development of respiratory disease and lowering mortality rates.

Air purifiers are very popular in the home. Now you know you can access your very own air purifier through the trees in your backyard and local parks.

The bottom line is that trees in urban landscapes contribute to cleaner air and more oxygen. We need more trees to help this process, especially large trees. Improving urban air quality through increasing the tree canopy in cities benefits everyone. Researchers have even identified the best trees for improving urban air quality, including silver birch, yew and elder, red maple, and conifers such as pine and cypress. Let's celebrate by remembering the International Day of Clean Air for Blue Skies on 7 September.

Does your local council have a plan to encourage greater tree canopy? Which trees would be best suited for where you live?

If you have a garden and have the room, add some trees that suit your location. Some useful plants for your home and office that produce oxygen and remove toxins include the spider plant, peace lily, golden cane palm, philodendron, variegated snake plant, areca palm, dracena, aloe vera, pineapple fern, Boston fern, golden pothos, flamingo lily, bamboo palm, weeping fig, rubber plant and gerbera. (My favourite is the trusty 'swiss cheese plant'. It's almost indestructible.) Or, you could add some extra plants to the back veranda or balcony in pots or hanging baskets, such as perennial geraniums, curry leaf tree, rosemary, basil, desert rose or sansevieria (mother-in-law's tongue).

Why not chat to your local garden nursery to see which plants would be best suited for your location and which are toddler- and pet-friendly?

Trees help keep us cool

Trees not only reduce the impact of air pollution, they also help cool our urban environments.

Kings Park and Botanic Garden in Perth, Western Australia, is one of the world's largest and most beautiful inner-city parks. (OK, I may be a little biased, but it's true.) Covering over

400 hectares, two-thirds of the park is bushland, providing the local population and visitors with clean, cool air.

You've probably noticed heat radiating from building surfaces and the ground on hot days. Concrete, bricks and asphalt absorb more heat than natural surfaces, creating what is called the 'urban heat island effect'. Adding sufficient tree canopy helps keep our homes and buildings cooler and reduces energy bills by providing shade and evapotranspiration.

Many city buildings now have rooftop gardens that are not only attractive to look at but also reduce stormwater runoff, increase biodiversity, and lower the roof surface temperature and the ambient city temperature by up to 4 degrees Celsius. Examples include Chicago's City Hall; Namba Parks, a retail and office complex in Osaka, Japan, which has an eight-level rooftop garden complete with waterfalls; the California Academy of Sciences in San Francisco; and the six-acre green roof of the Vancouver Convention Centre. Around the world, London and Tokyo have the most rooftop gardens that are open to the public, closely followed by Singapore and New York.

Another way of greening our urban areas is green laneways. Montreal, Canada, has 346 green laneways or 'ruelles vertes', created through a community-led program to improve environmental conditions and bring communities together. Similarly, Toronto has its Laneway Project, a social enterprise bringing green space to areas underserved by parks. In Melbourne, Australia, green laneways have been popping up since the city began handing out greening permits to residents and businesses; previously rather sad-looking grotty areas, full of rubbish, have been transformed into attractive, healthier and cooler places that are also attracting more birdlife.

Liverpool in the UK and cities in Spain, Portugal and the Netherlands have received funding for green projects to make cities cleaner (with better air quality) and greener. In 2019, Liverpool City Council hosted a pop-up forest to raise awareness and understanding of the benefits of urban green space. Locals were invited to visit and enjoy a brief experience of the tranquillity of being in a forest while in a city centre.

Beyond pop-ups, how about creating your own tiny urban forest? All you need is some land roughly 10 square metres in size. First devised by Akira Miyawaki, Japanese micro-forests are being used in urban environments to restore biodiversity and mitigate the urban heat island effect. Through careful planning, preparation and planting, these tiny forests grow ten times faster, become 30 times denser (because of dense planting) and are 100 times more biodiverse than regular forests. Australian National University Professor of Forestry Peter Kanowski believes micro-forests have the potential to lower urban temperatures, which will benefit urban residents and their communities.

Time to get shady

If you've ever stood at a suburban bus stop, you will know how hot you get standing on the pavement in full sun, with the radiant heat from nearby buildings and the road adding to your discomfort. Similarly, when waiting to cross the road at busy junctions, you'll see pedestrians sheltering under nearby shop canopies, if present, waiting for the little green man signal telling them it's safe to cross. We intuitively seek shade.

We need more urban green spaces and street trees to provide shelter, reduce glare and lower ambient temperature through shade and evapotranspiration. This works by transferring moisture from the earth into the atmosphere, similar to how we sweat. As the sweat evaporates from your skin, it cools you down. Similarly, when the sun's rays hit the top of the tree canopy, more water evaporates from their leaves, reducing the amount of energy left to heat the surrounding air.

One large oak tree can transpire over 150,000 litres of water a year! With 50% tree cover, the cooling effect, which is maximal in the afternoon, can be in the order of 1.8 degrees Celsius.

While you might have to wait a while for a tree to grow sufficiently big to exert its cooling effect, bushes, shrubs and long grasses also help. This is where selecting plants to create natural shade, such as vines, will help keep you cool and help reduce the chance of burning your feet from walking barefoot on hot concrete or tarmac.

Tree planting isn't a solution for everyone or everywhere, but retaining green and blue spaces in urban areas matters. Action requires everyone's input. Less concrete and more trees and green vegetation, and adequate water supply, will create more pleasant, green, liveable cities.

The 3-30-300 rule can also help improve and expand local urban forests. It suggests that three decent-sized trees be visible from every home, every neighbourhood have a minimum 30% tree canopy, and everyone live 300 metres from the nearest accessible green space.

Professor Astell-Burt and his team have shown that 30% tree canopy is the threshold to ensure residents' better health and well-being. Some of the world's best green cities, including Barcelona, Bristol, Canberra, Seattle, Vancouver and Singapore, are great sources of inspiration for what is achievable.

Sydney aims to increase its urban tree canopy to 40% by 2036, though private households and building owners must make a significant contribution to achieve this. London is aiming higher with the goal of turning 50% of its urban spaces green by 2050. These are lofty goals that aim to breathe new life and health into our cities.

When is the best time to plant a tree? According to an old proverb, the best time was 20 years ago. The second-best time is now.

What will you be planting?

In a nutshell

- Air pollution is the world's single most significant environmental cause of preventable disease and premature death. This is a huge problem in our increasingly urbanised world. We can help tackle this by planting more trees.
- Leaves produce oxygen, which is essential for breathing, as well as filtering harmful particulate matter in the air around us.
- Trees also help cool our urban environments through shade and evapotranspiration, counteracting the 'urban heat island effect' found in many cities. Rooftop gardens and green laneways are not only attractive, they also reduce stormwater runoff, increase biodiversity and lower ambient city temperature.

Chapter 8

Sunshine

'Second only to fresh air, however, I should be inclined to rank light in importance for the sick. Direct sunlight, not only daylight, is necessary for a speedy recovery.'
– Florence Nightingale

Climbing a mountain had never been on my bucket list. When my husband suggested we go on a trip to Sabah in Malaysia, including climbing Mt Kinabalu, I was far more interested in seeing orangutans in the wild than standing on a mountaintop.

But then, there we were, with our head torches on, standing in the dark at the summit, 4095 metres above sea level, waiting for the sun to rise. It was worth the wait as long, gentle fingers of sunlight spread towards us, caressing the tops of the surrounding mountains and turning them from deep indigo to multiple shades of blue, pink, magenta and gold as we heralded a new day.

It was one of the most spectacular sunrises I've ever seen and certainly one of the most memorable.

Which is your favourite time of day? Is it the early morning, late afternoon or somewhere in between? Do you enjoy watching a sunrise or sunset?

Sunlight is essential to life. But what is it about sunlight that makes us feel so good? How does sunlight boost our mood, and what role does it play in keeping us healthy and well, and lowering inflammation?

*

Fresh air and sunshine have long been the recipe used to promote better health.

I have a lovely photograph of my father as an infant, wearing his warm bonnet, sitting up in his perambulator while his doting older sister looks on.

It was customary in that era for babies to be parked outside shopfronts or the front door of the home so mothers could get on with their chores and housework. Dr Luther Emmett Holt, a paediatrician, proposed the idea of 'airing' babies in his 1894 book *The Care and Feeding of Children: A catechism for the use of mothers and children's nurses* to renew and purify their blood and keep them strong.

The 1920s and 1930s were also the days of baby cages hung outside windows for the same reason. Thankfully, these soon went out of fashion. However, it remains common practice for Scandinavian parents today to leave their children outside for their nap, even when the outside temperatures are below freezing. In Swedish day care centres, you'll see rows of babies and toddlers sleeping outside at lunchtime.

It's believed that spending more time outside during the day keeps the children healthier, prevents them from catching as many coughs and colds, and helps them sleep better. While it's hard to find much research to back this up, have you ever slept better after spending more time outside during the day?

Visit a café with outdoor seating, and if it's hot you'll see many customers sitting in the sunshine or under a shade while they sip their coffee – not for a tan or necessarily because of a conscious decision to top up their vitamin D levels, but simply to feel the sun's warmth on their skin and the breeze in their hair. It feels good.

Growing up in the UK, we often had many consecutive months of low grey skies and drizzle, which may explain the rare phenomenon of seeing a multitude of Brits rushing outside in their work breaks on a beautiful sunny day to lie or sit on something green, stripping off shirts in gay abandon, soaking up the sun's rays, and going home a lovely shade of salmon pink. The incessant greyness also explains my love of Australia's clear blue skies and abundant sunshine.

Morning sunlight improves sleep

The earth's rotation every 24 hours led to the evolution of circadian rhythms that influence almost all life forms on Earth. This has given us an internal mechanism to synchronise our physiology with the outside world. More than that, every single cell in our body has its own internal clock, meaning we are subconsciously driven to follow this rhythm.

But somewhere along the line, through the introduction of artificial light and digital gadgets, we've ended up out of sync, our normal rhythm disrupted. This is believed to be contributing to the rising tide of mental and chronic stress-related health issues.

From a personal perspective, working night shifts as a doctor played havoc with my sleep patterns. While I no longer do shift work (thank heavens), I struggle big time with jetlag, especially after flying east, because my body is confused about whether I should be awake, asleep or eating!

If you're one of the 10% to 30% of individuals worldwide who struggle with sleep, getting enough good light at the right time of day is an important factor towards solving the problem. Whether you're a morning person or not, there are distinct advantages to getting out into bright sunlight after waking up, particularly for your mental health.

Why early morning light? Sunlight signals to your brain that it's time to wake up. Because light can penetrate your eyelids, this stimulates special melanopsin cells in the back of the eye that then signal your central biological clock, the tiny rice-sized suprachiasmatic nucleus (SCN) in the brain's hypothalamus, to produce more serotonin and a nice boost of cortisol, and stop the production of melatonin. This is where blue light plays a positive role in helping you know it's morning time. Your internal timer then prompts melatonin to be produced again in 16 hours' time to help keep you asleep. Ensuring that you're in bed in 16 hours, preparing for sleep and not working late on your computer, checking emails or watching that extra episode of your current favourite Netflix series, makes it easier to restore better sleep patterns.

As Nathaniel Watson, sleep specialist and Professor of Neurology at the University of Washington School of Medicine, reminds us, 'Light is the single most important element for setting our circadian clock, or internal 24-hour rhythm, and morning light is key'. It's external light that matters; staying inside with the lights on or going straight to a computer screen doesn't have the same effect.

If you can't get outside first thing, try to get outside within the first hour of being awake (assuming it's light where you are) and look for ways to get as much natural light into your eyes between 8 a.m. and noon as possible. We need at least 30 minutes of 1000 lux of sunlight to kickstart the circadian process, which is what you'll get from being outside, even on an overcast day. Bright sunny days can provide up to 100,000 lux!

While good sleep hygiene practices and consistent sleep times help us sleep better, early morning light exposure matters the most. You are probably aware that too much light exposure (especially blue) at night can hinder sleep, but it's important to remember the need for more natural light in the morning. Remember, your best night's sleep starts in the morning! However, if you love watching the sun rise or set, this is a perfect activity for synchronising your body clock.

Disruption of the circadian rhythm and poor sleep affect the release of other hormones that impact appetite and metabolism. It can also lead to problems with mood and cognitive performance and a higher risk of developing type 2 diabetes, obesity and metabolism dysfunction.

Camping in the backyard for a better night's sleep

When my friend Sarah, who lives in the UK, was struggling with insomnia and work-related stress, she decided to try sleeping in a tent in her back garden for a while. Luckily, her home is in a relatively light-pollution-free area. Naturally, when her kids saw what she was up to, they all wanted to join Mummy in the tent, resulting in the whole family and the dog sleeping in the garden.

Prior to the introduction of air conditioning in Australia, hot summer nights and poorly insulated homes contributed to a culture of sleeping in what was called the 'sleep-out', a partially enclosed area at the back of the house or on the back veranda, which was open to the elements and where you could catch some cooler night air.

Does time in nature help you sleep better? The research suggests it does.

When our kids were young, we went on many camping holidays. Cosy in our sleeping bags and tents, we were often tucked up ready for sleep far earlier than we would be at home, and would sleep soundly until dawn.

The reasons for this included the following:

- We ate dinner earlier, aiming to have prepped and cooked the meal before darkness fell. We were ready for bed by 8.30 p.m.!
- We were 'off-grid'; we had head torches to help us get around but no other distractions other than a book to wind down with.
- All that fresh air and tramping made us deliciously physically tired and more mentally relaxed. We weren't worrying about work-related issues.

Studies have shown how even a weekend away under canvas can lead to melatonin levels rising 1.4 hours earlier (melatonin is vital for helping you stay asleep) and a 69% shift in circadian timing.

Integrative physiologist Ken Wright from the University of Colorado Boulder showed how campers on a week-long trip were exposed to 13 times more natural light than at home, went to bed earlier, slept longer and saw their melatonin levels rise 2.6 hours earlier than usual by the end of the week.

But even if camping is not your thing, time outside in nature and getting more early morning light will set you up for a better night's sleep.

Green noise can also enhance sleep – sounds found in natural environments, like rustling leaves or the sound of rain. These are lower-frequency sounds that can mask other unwanted sounds (like your partner snoring) and promote delta-wave brain activity associated with deep sleep and relaxation.

My husband and I once camped close to the side of a raging river so loud that it was like sitting next to a 747 aircraft. Amazingly, we slept like babies, lulled by the deafening roar only a few metres away.

Of course, not all natural sounds are conducive to sleep, like the time a wild camel chose to empty its bladder outside my tent!

Listening to green noise either in a natural environment or on an app has become a popular way of enhancing better sleep, especially for those dealing with anxiety and stress. What matters is finding the right sound for you.

More sunlight, less depression

Bright days and dark nights are best for mental health.

Spending time outside in sunlight boosts the release of the neurotransmitter serotonin. While serotonin is primarily produced in your gut, your serotonin levels get a nice top-up when you spend time outside. Serotonin helps you feel calm, positive and focused. You also feel more energised. This is why if you spend too much time indoors and feel sluggish, getting outside can be a real pick-me-up.

As a self-confessed serotonin seeker, I know the day I spend time outside will always be a good day. While too much time in the sun can be detrimental, leading to sunburn, premature skin ageing (yikes!) or heat stress, getting enough natural sunlight, especially in the early morning, provides many health benefits.

Seasonal affective disorder (SAD) affects some people living at certain latitudes where the amount of available daylight is limited. This type of depression is helped with bright-light therapy in the form of a lightbox. SAD lamps are designed to mimic sunlight, providing a minimum of 10,000 lumens, and are to be used for 20 to 30 minutes before 8 a.m. Some also mimic sunrise, gradually getting brighter as you wake up.

Light-based therapies are also used to boost work performance and circadian sleep-wake disorders. Individuals with disturbed sleep patterns, such as those with Alzheimer's disease, also benefit from these types of treatments. Ultraviolet light stimulates the skin's production of beta-endorphins, which provide a feeling of well-being, boost the immune system, relieve pain and promote relaxation, wound healing, cellular differentiation and job satisfaction. Nice.

Sunlight also helps reduce liver inflammation and speeds up metabolism. That's because sunlight increases nitric oxide levels in the body, which helps to relax and dilate blood vessels. While sunlight won't help you lose weight, your improved health and well-being helps you to engage in healthier eating patterns, be more physically active and sleep better.

If you've always found that sunlight lifts your mood, the even better news is that a UK study of over 400,000 people showed the average participant spent 2.5 hours outside, and for every extra hour spent outside there was a significantly lower lifetime risk of major depressive disorder, use of antidepressants, low mood or neuroticism. In addition, each hour of daytime light was associated with finding it easier to get up, less frequent tiredness, fewer symptoms of insomnia and a greater inclination to rise early.

Healthy circadian rhythms are essential to mental health and well-being. One study of 86,772 people demonstrated how too much unhealthy night-time light exposure was associated with an increased risk of major depression, generalised anxiety disorder, PTSD, psychosis, bipolar disorder and self-harm.

What is unhealthy night-time light exposure? Bright indoor or outside lights after dark. So, let's get smarter at reducing unhealthy night light:

- Where possible, turn the lights off or use a dimmer switch.
- Aim to stop using any technology at least 60 minutes before you want to go to bed. This includes smartphones, laptops, tablets and TV screens.
- Get rid of gadgets with LED and LCD lights, like alarm clocks and radios.
- Choose warm light instead of bright white for your rooms, unless you plan to perform nocturnal surgery on your dining room table.
- The best nightlights for children use red light.

Associate Professor Sean Cain, a circadian biologist from Monash University, suggests we use the circadian rhythm 'as a simple, freely available, non-pharmacological intervention to enhance mental health that is easily implementable in a community setting'.

In the 1960s, it was thought that depression was caused by low serotonin levels, and it was described as a 'chemical imbalance'. This led to a flurry of new antidepressants, the selective serotonin reuptake inhibitors (SSRIs), being released onto the market in the 1980s. However, these drugs were only effective in some patients.

Today, after multiple studies, there is no clear evidence that low serotonin levels cause or are associated with depression.

While we don't have all the answers to what causes depression yet, it's the quality and quantity of our sleep, diet, level of physical activity and stress-reducing interventions that affect the level of inflammation in our bodies, which impact how the brain is wired and functions. In other words, it's lifestyle. Tuning in to what supports you to function at your best, including time in nature, is the key.

Sunlight is good for your body, too

If you were given the choice of a chef-run café producing beautiful meals at work or access to consistent natural light in your workspace, what would you choose? Yes, I'd like both, too, but which do you think would have the greatest impact on your happiness?

Surveys have shown that having access to natural light and views of green spaces matters more to workplace health and happiness than access to barista coffee, on-site childcare and chef-run cafés. Natural light was reported to boost happiness and well-being by 78%, work performance by 70%, work satisfaction by 73% and organisational commitment by 54%. In addition, studies by Cornell University showed how optimising natural light in workplaces reduced eyestrain by 51%, headaches by 63% and drowsiness by 56%.

Increased exposure to sunlight is associated with lower levels of perceived stress. Since sunlight is essential for producing vitamin D, the association between increased sun exposure and low levels of perceived stress is believed to be influenced by vitamin D levels. Vitamin D provides multiple protective factors, including supporting the immune system, brain health and reducing inflammation. Let's take a closer look at this remarkable vitamin.

Vitamin D is wrongly named, as it is a hormone. Every cell in your body has vitamin D receptors, and most of your cells can convert it to its active form to assist in cell processes. You obtain 90% of your vitamin D from UVB exposure and 10% from your food and supplements. It helps your body absorb and retain calcium and phosphate needed for strong muscles and bones. It's also vital in childhood for proper lung development, immune function and lung function. However, we don't know how much time children need to spend in the sun to achieve the protective effects while avoiding the downsides of too much sun exposure.

Too much sun exposure is potentially harmful. However, too little UV exposure leads to a greater risk of a higher disease burden of musculoskeletal disorders, including rickets, osteomalacia and osteoporosis, certain autoimmune disorders, and cancer of the lung, colon and breast.

In Australia, 5 to 15 minutes of sunlight on your arms, hands and face two to three times a week is enough for most of us. This is without applying sunscreen or wearing sunglasses. However, if you're over the age of 65, you'll produce only 25% of the vitamin D that younger adults do. Check UV levels at myuv.com.au.

In the UK, ten minutes daily between 11 a.m. and 3 p.m. is sufficient in the summer months, but you may need longer on cloudy days. The rule of thumb is if your shadow (outside) is longer than your height, your body is unlikely to be able to produce sufficient vitamin D from sunlight.

In a nutshell

- Morning sunlight is an important ingredient for good sleep. It lets your body know that it's time to wake up, setting your internal timer and keeping your circadian rhythm in sync.

- Sunlight has also been shown to help combat depression. It boosts serotonin, the feel-good neurotransmitter.
- Sunlight also contributes to your overall health and well-being in other ways, such as helping to reduce liver inflammation and speed up metabolism.
- Beware, though – overexposure to sunlight can be harmful. Always make sure to take the necessary precautions, such as applying sunscreen, wearing sunglasses and checking UV levels.

Chapter 9

Water

'I will do water – beautiful, blue water.' – Claude Monet

'Thousands have lived without love, not one without water.'
– WH Auden

'We must swim!'

The urgency in my German penfriend's voice was a perfect counterpoint to my total lack of enthusiasm.

We were standing on the flinty shoreline of Worthing Beach on a cold January morning, surrounded by low grey clouds, loud squawking seagulls laughing at us, and a miserable-looking, choppy grey sea. She had to be joking, right?

She wasn't. Stripping off her clothes, she waded into the sea in her undies, calling out to me, 'Come on!'

After a few minutes of squealing and squawking, making even more noise than the gulls, Susie admitted it was cold. With teeth chattering and blue hands and lips, we dried ourselves as best we could and quickly returned to my grandfather's house for a hot shower.

Susie had never seen the sea before.

*

A small tributary of the Camel River in Cornwall runs through the bottom of my parents' former garden. I used to love standing on the small wooden bridge separating the garden from some natural woodland perfect for playing Poohsticks*. It is a true *Wind in the Willows* place where you can imagine Toad and Mole engaged in conversation. From the bridge, you could watch how the flowing water shaped and changed the riverbank, building it up in some places and eroding it in others.

Standing on the bridge and watching the water made me think about how we are like water in many ways: adaptive, persistent, and super resilient. When we encounter an obstacle, we look for a way to work around it, just as water finds a way around a fallen tree branch or large rock.

When the river flooded – which it did, not infrequently – seeing the force of the water pushing debris along in its wake was worrying. Then, after it all subsided, the gentleness of the flow once more caressed the reeds and grasses – just like the ebb and flow of life.

Nature has many ways of showing us that resilience is about finding a way forward through the good and bad times.

*

Like sunlight and oxygen, we need water to survive. Along with every other living being, we depend on water to sustain us. We can go without food for a while, but we can only survive without water for a few days, or even less if we are in a hot environment.

---

* 'Poohsticks' is a game created by Winnie-the-Pooh after he noticed how, after accidentally dropping a fir cone off a bridge into a river, it popped up again on the other side. To play, you need one or more people and a stick per person, which are simultaneously dropped off the edge of a bridge into a river. The winner is the person whose stick appears first on the other side. It's hours of fun. Thanks go to A.A. Milne, author of *The House at Pooh Corner*.

We are water. As David Suzuki so eloquently reminds us, 'We are over 60 percent water by weight. We're just a big ... blob of water, with enough organic thickener added so we don't dribble away on the floor'. Is that why we are drawn to be near water or immerse ourselves in it, or to pay more for a property with a water view? Is that why we feel inspired, calmed and restored by it?

Do you like the idea of a romantic dinner for two overlooking the ocean or on a beach? *Yes, please.* What about a brisk, windy walk along a coastal cliff where you can look down onto the rocks, marvelling at the power of the waves and the multitude of shades of blue, green and frothy white seafoam? *I'll grab my jacket.* Or, how about cruising a fjord and witnessing a majestic waterfall cascading hundreds of metres to the ocean below? *Where do I sign up?*

Michael Phelps, a former American competitive swimmer and the most successful Olympian of all time, with 28 gold medals to his name, explains the feeling as, 'I feel most at home in the water. I disappear. That's where I belong'.

With 1.16 million kilometres of coastline available, there is plenty of space for all. With 40% of the world's population living within 100 km of the coast, according to the United Nations, it's clearly something we as a species like to spend time with.

The mental health benefits of water

There's something about being close to water that is especially meditative. Pictures of beautiful blue and green spaces evoke greater positive feelings than urban scenes, but water images are preferred and reported as more calming.

Marine biologist Dr Wallace Nichols, author of *Blue Mind*, describes the effect of being in a blue space as 'a mildly meditative state characterised by calm, peacefulness, unity, and a sense of general happiness and satisfaction'. In case you were wondering, blue space is any visible natural or artificial surface water, including rivers, waterfalls, lakes, oceans, ponds and fountains.

You may have noticed how well you sleep after spending time outdoors in a blue space. All that salty sea air exerts a powerful effect, with one small study conducted by the UK National Trust showing that walking by the sea can lengthen sleep time by up to 47 minutes. Walking anywhere outside in nature reduces stress and nurtures relaxation.

A UK study of 20,000 smartphone users who tracked their environment and sense of well-being at random intervals found that people living closer to marine or coastal areas were significantly happier than those living in urban areas. Another study conducted in Wellington, New Zealand, showed that residents living in neighbourhoods with increased blue space views (predominantly of the ocean) experienced lower levels of psychological distress.

Does this mean you must be wealthy enough to live closer to a blue space to be happier? Actually, no. Work done by the University of Exeter has revealed that the positive relationship between living in a more natural environment and better mental health is stronger among more socioeconomically disadvantaged populations.

Coastal environments and living within 1 km of water do appear to provide a mental health resource. Of those living close to water, 22% of individuals were shown to be at less risk of developing anxiety or depression compared to those living 50 km away from the coast.

Living and working in a city can mean your access to a blue space might be highly variable. However, a regular 20-minute walk around a blue space – whether it's a fountain, water feature, pond or lake – will boost well-being and mood by triggering the release of serotonin and endorphins.

Waves of Wellness (WOW) was co-founded by Joel Pilgrim, a mental health occupational therapist and long-time surfer passionate about helping young people deal with and recover from mental health challenges. I chatted with Heather, WOW's general manager, who explained what makes the WOW surfing experiences work so well:

- Being outside in a blue space – the beach is less intimidating than receiving therapy one-on-one in a grey room in a building.
- You are part of a small, intimate group of ten, meaning you discover you're not alone in your experience or recovery, and you're in a safe space with two mental health professionals.
- You're being active and learning a new life skill, which is also fun.
- You're learning alongside others; there's no judgment.
- The sessions build confidence and self-efficacy.
- As your skills improve, you're motivated to keep attending because you feel good and know you're achieving something special.

As Heather says, being on, in or beside water provides us with different perspectives and builds resilience in dealing with life's challenges.

Many similar programs are offering these types of therapies. Better still, many are not-for-profit and provided free to participants. Referrals to the WOW program come from GPs, schools and self-referrals, and 50% are from word-of-mouth, the best form of referral of all.

Some workplaces also sign up for a four-week program as part of a mental health well-being strategy. In this program, everyone participates as an equal and shares a common language.

The physical health benefits of water

We know of the relationship between increased physical activity and better mental health. Well, living near or having easy access to a blue space is linked to a greater probability of being more physically active, whether swimming or walking.

I have always enjoyed visiting places with water views but had never really appreciated the joy of being immersed in water until I learnt to swim as an adult. The reason I did this was I had chronic neck and shoulder pain that my physiotherapist clearly felt needed other management than my occasional visits to her clinic for massage and ultrasound.

'I suggest you go swimming regularly', she said. She wasn't the kind of person you argue with, so I found myself a swimming coach who specialised in teaching adults like me how to swim correctly.

I soon discovered the bliss of diving into a pool, and once I had learnt how to coordinate my breathing with the rhythm of the stroke so as not to swallow half the pool's water, I began to enjoy the meditative quality of following that black line. Within a couple of weeks, my chronic pain had melted away, but now I was also fitter, stronger, healthier and happier.

Research has shown swimming is the perfect body and mind workout. It is accessible to people of all ages and levels of ability, including those with physical limitations. It boosts heart, lung, brain and mental health and lowers inflammation in the body through:

- increased lung capacity
- stronger heart muscle
- lower blood pressure
- improved muscle strength and tone
- improved insulin sensitivity and blood glucose management

- reduced joint pain and enhanced flexibility, including for people with arthritis.

It even slows down the ageing process.

My favourite pool is a public 50-metre outdoor pool surrounded by trees that cast their lengthening shadows over the water in the afternoon. I try to access a lane that retains the sunlight for the longest time. It's a beautiful space that makes me feel good by just being there.

What do you connect with water for? Is it for exercise, relaxation or play? In her book *Why We Swim*, Bonnie Tsui discusses the many reasons for swimming, from survival to competition, therapy and health. I've certainly encountered many people who swim or interact with water for all those reasons.

Whatever your reason, do what's right for you and is safe, not just the latest fad. Even if you hate swimming or getting your hair wet, there are many other water-based activities to choose from. Surfing, bodyboarding, paddleboarding, kayaking and kitesurfing are all immensely popular ways of enjoying the water.

My friend Doug attributes much of his recovery from cancer to being able to access water:

> I had a large lipo-sarcoma removed from my left buttock in late 2008. The tumour was wrapped around my sciatic nerve. The nerve was excised in the removal process, and I was left with no motor control, no muscles and very little feeling below my left knee. I was fitted with an ankle-foot orthotic and learned how to walk again.
>
> Before the sarcoma, I had always been keen on various forms of outdoor exercise, some of which, like running, I could no longer do.
>
> I thought paddling a kayak might be an option. I modified the pedals of my sit-on-top kayak and took it down

to the river. It was a windy day, and the kayak was in poor condition. The outing was not very successful. I later found a better stretch of river and started paddling there occasionally.

I purchased a slightly more advanced kayak, and a friend told me about a group that met early on Saturday mornings. I discovered the weekly routine was a short race and a training session. I immediately became part of the group and have been at every Saturday morning event, since Perth is blessed with extensive, useable, varied stretches of recreational water. Being able to leave the suburbs or the workplace and become part of a wilderness environment in the middle of town is very settling for one's temperament. Most training sessions occur early in the morning, and I love witnessing the sunrise.

The time spent in the pristine outdoor environment and the social interaction that comes with it are additional constant benefits to my well-being.

Surfing is one of the fastest-growing aquatic sports. Surfing and other water-based championships bring competitors and observers from all over the world to the events, and some of the competitors are there not just to compete but also for their own healing and health. The Australian Lifesaving culture began in Sydney, with the first club founded at Bondi in 1907. Since then, countless kids and grown-ups have volunteered to keep swimmers and beachgoers safe, patrolling popular swim beaches and undertaking training to obtain their proficiency surf bronze medallion. In Perth, the annual Rottnest Channel Swim from Cottesloe Beach to Rottnest Island is 19.7 km and open to teams of four, two or solo swimmers with their support crew of boats and kayaks. It's a swim undertaken for personal reasons to show you can improve your best time or participate in a fun team event for a worthy cause.

I've always wished I could be like Ariel, the little mermaid, but my childhood history of asthma and inability to equalise has always precluded me from learning to dive. However, I love snorkelling and seeing the extraordinary variety of sea creatures and plants that live below the surface. While sometimes nervous on the ocean's surface, my fear melts away when wearing a snorkel mask or goggles, turning to curiosity and wonder.

One of the greatest benefits of our revived love of spending time in the water has been the growing awareness of the need to keep our waterways and oceans clean. The Seine River, which runs through Paris, was closed for public swimming for 100 years, but with the 2024 Summer Olympics in Paris, much work was undertaken to make the river safe again. Hurrah! Other urban river swimming spots include Basel and Zurich in Switzerland, while in New York there is a plus-shaped pool designed to filter 600,000 gallons of water each day to leave safe, swimmable river water. My hope is that one day there will be more safe and swimmable urban rivers.

One of my friends was lucky enough to visit the Galapagos Islands a few years ago. It was the trip of a lifetime, but the highlight for her wasn't the islands and seeing the sea lizards that live there; it was the opportunity to take a deep dive and watch a group of approximately 200 hammerhead sharks cruise lazily in a circle close to the surface while the diving group stayed below!

We can all create our own unique blue space experiences. Swimming with hammerhead sharks will not be one of mine.

The benefits of cold exposure

Since moving to Australia, I have adapted to the hot summers and mild winters. Frosts are rare, and snow falls only in a few isolated areas. I have grown accustomed to our warm climate and love it.

I confess to being a bit surprised by the rapid uptake of cold-water immersion in Australia and around the world. My husband has always teased me about my refusal to enter the water unless the ambient temperature is at least 28 degrees Celsius. A cold-water challenge to raise money for charity is one thing, but willingly jumping into an ice bath or choosing only to take cold-water showers is another. Have we all been seduced by the Wim Hof method?

Cold-water immersion has been practised for centuries by those living in the Nordic countries. It's not for the faint-hearted, and if you, like me, are not a polar bear, you might be wondering, *Is this really something I should be doing too?* Why have we all gone crazy about cold-water immersion, outside swimming and cold showers?

The fans of cold-water immersion wax loud and lyrical about the vitality-bringing qualities of the cold shock to your system. However, like anything, it's about working out what is suitable (and safe) for you. There is now a growing library of research supporting its use. If it appeals and you want to try it, this is what is important to know.

Take caution, though. It's known that cold exposure can kill. The tawdry tale of Francis Bacon, who died from pneumonia in 1626 shortly after stuffing a chicken with snow to see if it would preserve the flesh, is a lesson to us all. Immersion deaths are the third most common cause of accidental death in adults, and second in children. Mike Tipton, Professor of Human and Applied Physiology at the University of Portsmouth and head of the Environmental Medicine Division at the Institute of Naval Medicine in the UK, dentified that the initial cold shock can trigger cardiac arrythmias.

A 2023 study found that whole-body cold-water immersion (keeping your head up) produces a physiological response that makes you more active, alert, attentive, inspired and proud of your achievement, and less nervous or distressed. This is the response that makes you say, 'That was grand, I feel so alive!'

Even a short single exposure to cold water triggers a cascade of adaptive reactions that are beneficial to the immune system, reducing inflammation and fatigue, lessening symptoms of depression and improving general well-being. In addition, a whole raft of neurotransmitters, including serotonin, dopamine, cortisol, norepinephrine and beta-endorphins, are released, assisting in emotional and stress regulation and reward processing. This is why cold-water immersion helps with depression, anxiety and psychological distress.

If it's something you're keen to try, this is the recommended way to try cold-water therapy:

1. If you're over 40, check you're fit enough to do this. Remember you're initiating a shock to your system, so there are no brownie points for giving yourself a heart attack. Chat to your GP before you do it, especially if you're on medications like beta blockers or have an underlying heart condition.

2. Always – as in, every time – make sure you have someone else with you. Think of it like any other outdoor adventure. There is safety in numbers.

3. Voluntarily enter cold water for several minutes and have a brief swim. Start slowly and build up from a few seconds to longer. You can acclimatise first by getting used to having cooler showers, doing other forms of exercise outside in cooler weather and trying less severe cold-water swims.

Stay in the water for a couple of minutes. The colder the water, the shorter the time.

4. You can get all scientific and measure the temperature of the water or be guided by how it feels: if it feels too cold, it probably is. The water temperature of an indoor swimming pool is typically between 26 and 31 degrees Celsius. When starting out, the suggestion is to go when the water is about 15 degrees Celsius or above to get used to it. Anything less that will feel 'a bit nippy', 'chilly' or possibly 'bloody freezing'.

5. The key is to immerse yourself gently. Don't dive in. Be prepared for the shock. You might gasp or say something very loudly like, 'Sheeesh, that's cold!' That's because the shock to your system causes your blood pressure to drop and your heart rate to accelerate. Hyperventilation occurs for the first few seconds, putting you at risk of passing out. Keep your head above water, especially in those first few seconds.

6. Be prepared to prevent hypothermia. You might want to wear a beanie, neoprene booties and gloves, or even a wetsuit. With hypothermia, it gets harder to move or think, and everything slows down. A few years back I jumped into a New Zealand river fully clothed to rescue our young daughter after she capsized in her kayak. The shock of that glacial water took my breath away, but what shocked me more was how my body and mind didn't respond in the way I wanted them to. My daughter was brought to shore without any issue, but I became trapped on a submerged tree branch and, in those few minutes, expected to drown. The most significant risk of hypothermia setting in is after you get out of the water, especially if it's windy. So, after your swim, take it easy for an hour or two. Secondary hypothermia

causes a drop in blood pressure and heart rate and is difficult to recover from. Have a set of warm, dry clothes you can immediately change into, get into a warm space and have a hot drink.

If you want to learn more, the US National Center for Cold Water Safety website, coldwatersafety.org, has lots of useful advice.

The benefits of heat exposure

If you're not so keen on the cold, why not try it hot?

Spa therapy, hot springs, water-related healing landscapes and balneotherapy, which includes bathing in or drinking hot spring water or mineral water, have long been used for their circulation and health benefits. The perceived health benefits of water led to the development of spa baths by the Ancient Romans, such as the hot springs in the British spa town of Bath, which were used for bathing and drinking. Inclusivity then saw the introduction of the Bath Chair in 1750, invented by James Heath to allow the sick and infirm to access the healing waters. Today, thalassotherapy treatments (comprising warm seawater, algae, seaweed or alluvial mud) remain popular for enhancing well-being and treating various skin ailments. Sometimes, just having a lovely long soak in a hot bath at home is the perfect way to unwind and relax.

While there's not a great deal of research available to reveal the health benefits, one interesting discovery was that having a hot bath after 7 p.m. is associated with a 15% lower risk of hypertension for those over the age of 65. Other studies report it helps to reduce stress, enhance sleep and reduce symptoms of osteoarthritis and fibromyalgia. Balneotherapy is thought to improve psoriasis and atopic dermatitis by influencing the skin and gut microbiota. One small study looked at how unique mineral properties of different types of hot spring water modify the gut microbiome in specific ways. Watch this space as we learn more.

Hammams, or Turkish baths, have been used as a social hub for public bathing since the Ottoman Empire. If the thought of a very sudsy massage appeals, it could be just the ticket for unwinding after a busy week, overcoming jet lag or catching up with friends. Did I mention it's a hot and humid experience?

After stripping off and covering yourself with a towel, you wait until invited to enter the hot room, or *sıcaklık* (like a sauna). Then, you go to the belly stone, or *göbek taşı* – a raised platform where you lie on your belly and get your deep massage. Next, you move into the cold room, or *soğukluk*, to cool down before finishing up in the *kese* room to receive a traditional (slightly abrasive) Turkish scrub. If that appeals, try it out.

The Japanese culture of bathing in natural hot springs or *onsen* is considered the perfect pick-me-up after a long day. While communal naked bathing is less common in Western countries, the Japanese don't think twice about it, though it's common for men and women to take their *onsen* separately.

The *onsen* etiquette is simple:

1. Slip off your shoes and clothes in the changing room.
2. Next, take a shower by sitting on a low wooden stool in a communal washing space, washing your body with soap and rinsing off with water from a bowl.
3. Those using a modesty towel (the size of a flannel) then fold it up and put it on their head before entering the *onsen*.
4. Sit in the warm water and relax! The water can feel quite hot, so only bathe for short sessions and take a break every so often to allow your body to cool down. This is similar to the Nordic tradition of taking a hot sauna for 15 to 20 minutes followed by a cold plunge for 1 to 12 minutes.

Onsen may be available at different temperatures, so find the one you like best. After your *onsen*, why not enjoy a cup of Japanese tea?

There's something quite magical about sitting in a hot spring surrounded by forest or, in winter, the snow. I highly recommended it! Perhaps a hot bath a day does keep the doctor away!

In a nutshell

- Water is essential for human life. We are over 60% water.
- Water also provides mental health benefits. 'Blue spaces' have been found to have a calming effect. Research has also found that people who live near the coast are less likely to develop anxiety or depression.
- Visiting the coast or a waterway for a walk or to sit and watch the water is an ideal way to enjoy being in a blue space.
- Swimming is the perfect body and mind workout. It boosts heart, lung, brain and mental health, and it lowers inflammation in the body.
- Exposure to cold water reduces inflammation and fatigue, lessens symptoms of depression and improves general wellbeing, as well as releasing a whole raft of neurotransmitters that assist in emotional and stress regulation and reward processing.
- If that doesn't appeal, though, exposure to hot water also has health benefits including lowering risk of hypertension, improving sleep and reducing stress and symptoms of osteoporosis, fibromyalgia, psoriasis and atopic dermatitis.

Chapter 10

Earth

During World War II, Finland ceded a swath of its territory to Russia, splitting an area called Karelia into separate Finnish and Russian territories.

As with the establishment of the Berlin Wall, life on the two sides was very different. Those living on the Finnish side saw environmental and lifestyle changes through more urbanisation and improved living standards compared to the Russian side, which remained primarily rural. However, what happened next was the discovery that the Finnish population had a significantly higher prevalence of allergies than those living on the Russian side.

The question was, why?

Dr David Strachan, an epidemiologist, formulated what became known as the 'hygiene hypothesis' in 1989. He reported an inverse relationship between family size and the development of atopic or allergic disorders. In other words, younger siblings need older siblings to play with and get dirty. This created the idea that while it was good to be clean, being too clean was a potential health hazard.

Now we have the biodiversity hypothesis, which argues that a low level of biodiversity, and hence microbial diversity, can lead to the dysregulation of the human immune system.

Could our immune system, which includes our microbiome, depend on the calibration provided by nature's microbiome? In other words, does dirt directly contribute to human health?

The impact of dirt on our immune systems

The mind-blowing statistics estimate that 59% of the world's species live in the soil, along with 90% of all fungi, 85% of all plants and 50% of bacteria. One gram of soil contains about one kilometre of fungal filaments and a billion bacteria.

The human microbiome is found on our skin and in our gut, whereas the rhizosphere of soil acts like a plant's external gut. The process of photosynthesis releases sugars, 11% to 40% of which are pumped into the ground around the plant's roots to feed the local bacteria and allow them to proliferate. This is like how human breast milk, which contains sugars called oligosaccharides, feeds the bacteria in the baby's gut. Our gut bacteria protect us from pathogen invasion; a plant's immune system achieves the same outcome using bacteria in the rhizosphere.

Our better understanding of the gut–brain connection has led to the discovery that Parkinson's disease, among others, probably originates in the gut and is, in part, an autoimmune disease. Hippocrates stated 2000 years ago, 'All disease starts in the gut'; he wasn't right, but many chronic metabolic diseases do.

We depend on our immune system to keep us well and prevent disease. Numerous studies have shown that spending time in nature protects against a wide range of infectious and inflammatory conditions. However, how this works hasn't been well understood. Integrative Physiology Professor Christopher Lowry has spent over two decades investigating whether our urban environments contribute to our increasing rates of stress-related disease because we've lost the interconnection between ourselves and the microbes found in soil.

In 1971, British scientists noticed that a vaccine given to protect against tuberculosis produced a better response in residents of Lake Kyoga in Uganda than elsewhere. A microorganism called Mycobacterium vaccae was discovered in the soil on the lake's shoreline. It appeared to have an immune-regulating effect.

Following that discovery, other researchers attempted to use M. vaccae as an immune booster in other vaccines, but with little success. Then, in 2000, a UK study used killed M. vaccae in a small group of patients with inoperable and advanced lung cancer. While it made no difference to overall survival times, the patients' quality of life and mental health improved. This spurred Lowry and his team to investigate further.

In 2007, Lowry published a study showing how mice injected with heat-killed M. vaccae activated serotonin-producing neurons in the brain and altered their behaviour in a similar way to that shown in antidepressants. He later showed how injecting M. vaccae helped the mice be more stress-resilient before a stressful event.

Other human studies have shown that children raised in a rural environment surrounded by animals and lots of bacteria-laden dust have more stress-resilient immune systems in adulthood than their counterparts raised in urban areas without pets. It's also been shown that M. vaccae has a long-lasting anti-inflammatory effect on the brain. This may reduce anxiety, mood disorders and other neuroinflammatory conditions.

Does this mean we need to get our hands dirty more often to reduce our risk of mental illness? No, but it does go some way to explain why gardening can make us feel so good. Getting dirty isn't what helps our immune system; it's the diversity of our microbiome that counts. We need contact with soil that exposes us to a wide variety of microbes and worms – not just earthworms but all the other wrigglies, including millipedes and nematodes.

So, now we know: soil directly contributes to human health. Contact with the natural environment enriches the human microbiome, promotes the immune response, and protects you from allergies and inflammatory disorders.

Allergy and immune diseases currently affect one in five Australians, according to the Allergy and Immunology Foundation of Australasia (AIFA), which can significantly impact your quality of life. We need contact with our 'old friends', the bacteria and parasites in the natural environment, along with airborne volatile substances produced by terrestrial (forest) and marine vegetation. Non-infectious organisms act through the skin, as well as influencing the gut biome.

I might book that mud spa after all.

Bringing dirt into your day

If access to the outdoors is limited, it's time to get creative. Paddling pools, climbing frames, swings and slides are all great, but nothing beats a good mud kitchen.

Depending on your DIY prowess and budget, this can be anything you want it to be. Take one pre-loved table or chest of drawers, find an assortment of pots, pans and stirring utensils, a washing-up bowl, measuring spoons and a jug of water, and remember plenty of soil to make good mud. Your children will love it, and I suspect you'll have just as much fun watching or getting your own hands dirty. Mud pies are coming your way!

In a slightly unconventional study, Finnish researchers replaced the asphalt and gravel in the schoolyards of four day care centres with transplanted soil and vegetation taken from coniferous forests. They were also provided with planter boxes for gardening. Why? Well, if it's not possible to get the children into the forest, you bring the forest to the children. After four weeks, the children were found to have an increased diversity of skin and gut microbiome and improved immune function, with an increase in the proportion of anti-inflammatory molecules and increased T (white) cells in the blood.

In a nutshell

- Exposure to dirt can boost your immune system by improving the diversity of your microbiome. In particular, a microorganism called Mycobacterium vaccae, found in soil, has been found to have many beneficial properties, including a long-lasting anti-inflammatory effect on the brain that may reduce anxiety, mood disorders and other neuroinflammatory conditions.

- If access to the outdoors is limited, you need to bring dirt into your day. Mud kitchens are fun for the whole family, and replacing asphalt and gravel with planter boxes full of soil and vegetation can improve your skin and gut microbiome.

Chapter 11

Animals

'It seems to me that the natural world is the greatest source of excitement; the greatest source of visual beauty; the greatest source of intellectual interest. It is the greatest source of so much in life that makes life worth living.'
– Sir David Attenborough

Animals connect us to nature and may boost our mental health. For example, seeing or hearing birds, regardless of whether you can see other aspects of nature, has been shown to have a positive effect on everyone, including those recovering from depression.

In one study, 1292 participants were invited to submit their demographics, current mental well-being, and encounters with birds they could see or hear using the Urban Mind app. The study showed that seeing or hearing birds enhanced mental well-being, especially when the participants were outdoors, and the beneficial effect lasted for some time.

Do you know which species of birds are commonly found near your home? There may be more than you think. The North American continent is home to 2069 bird species, the UK has 628 and the state of Victoria in Australia has over 500.

My backyard is frequently visited by a variety of birds, including rosellas, magpies, crows, honeyeaters and kookaburras. The latter treat my veranda rail as the perfect spot for observing insects hovering over the shrubs. My favourite small bird is the male superb fairy-wren darting about showing off his beautiful iridescent blue plumage. Do you have a favourite?

It's not just about birdlife, though. Environments rich in all kinds of wildlife are associated with improved well-being, contributing to elevated self-esteem and mood.

Looking out for wildlife

'Oooooh look! It's an echidna!'

Fascinated, we stopped and peered at our newfound spiky friend, who took absolutely no notice of us as he or she (I don't know how you tell the difference) snuffled and scrabbled in the undergrowth, looking for breakfast. We walked on with big smiles on our faces, delighted by the experience and keeping our eyes peeled for what else we might see.

There's something rather special about seeing wildlife in their natural habitat. Whether they are dolphins, humpback whales, kangaroos, ducks, albatrosses, foxes or squirrels, seeing them provides us with joy. We're curious to observe them, often entertained by their antics and delighted by their presence, no matter how fleeting.

Many cities have zoos, enabling us to get up close and personal with many different creatures we might not otherwise ever have the opportunity to see. Thankfully, many of today's zoos are well designed to ensure the health and well-being of their residents.

There are also opportunities for human–wildlife interactions in our urban environments that provide mental, physical, social and spiritual benefits. As well as birds, I also have honeybees visiting my property from next door's hives, many butterflies and dragonflies, tiny geckos basking on the sunny side of my laundry wall, and the occasional blue-tongued lizard in our shrubbery.

The value of pets

Humans love pets. It's estimated there are 1 billion worldwide, with half of that number being cats and dogs residing in the US, Brazil, Europe and China. Australians clearly love their pets, too; we have one of the world's highest pet ownership rates, with around 28.7 million pets for our population of 26.6 million in 69% of households. Dogs account for 48% of Australian pets, with cats coming in second at 33%.

Our interactions with animals unconsciously boost compassion and kindness. If you've ever taken your kids to an animal farm, you'll have witnessed their joy at seeing, holding and petting all the different animals. Be warned, on the way home they'll be trying to persuade you that they desperately need their own pony, alpaca or lamb to care for.

It's been shown that children who do have pets develop a sense of responsibility and empathy for the animal. By learning how to care for and interact with the animal, they also develop the skills to socialise better with their human friends. If getting a pony isn't going to happen because of the high cost or the lack of an appropriate place to keep it (the backyard isn't usually the best option), a guinea pig or perhaps a goldfish might be a better place to start and a good way to test their level of commitment to caring for their pet.

A study of adolescents with type 1 diabetes showed how caring for animals boosts self-care. The teenagers were encouraged to look after some pet fish, which involved daily feeding, checking the tank's water level and changing the tank water each week. The result showed that the adolescents became more disciplined in monitoring their blood sugar levels. Could that be adapted for training your kids to empty the dishwasher and keep their bedrooms tidy?

Are pets the new probiotic? This was the question posed by an article in *The New York Times*. Knowing some of the disgusting things our dogs choose to try and eat, I can definitely say it's not a good idea to let your dog lick your face. Some people are allergic to animal dander or develop asthma around animals. Others aren't sure if pets are hygienic. However, children given early exposure to pets not only learn to interact with animals safely, they also gain a healthier microbiome linked to more robust immune function. The latest research suggests people with pets develop different microbiota in different areas of the human body, with lower levels of harmful (pathogenic) bacteria and an increase in beneficial bacteria.

Stroking a dog has been shown to raise levels of immunoglobulin A (IgA), which protects us from pathogens and forms a physical barrier in the gut. Not only that, if you are unfortunate enough to suffer a heart attack, your long-term survival rates are higher if you have a dog. If you have an elderly parent whose blood pressure is too high, having social interaction with an animal can help – even just 12 minutes of animal contact makes a difference.

It's also been shown that pregnant mothers who live with pets (mostly dogs and cats) are less likely to have infants with childhood allergies, asthma and obesity. Growing up surrounded by a veritable menagerie of assorted animals, thanks to my dad being a vet, protected me from two of these, but I was shown to be highly allergic to dust mites and dog and cat dander, so protection isn't guaranteed.

The human–dog bond

Domesticated around 30,000 years ago, dogs have long assisted humans with various tasks, such as hunting, retrieving, guarding and herding. The 2020 movie *The Truffle Hunters* beautifully portrays the dog–human relationship – the film introduces you to a small group of men living in the Piedmont region of northern Italy, whose closest relationship is clearly with their dogs rather than their wives!

Gazing into the eyes of your beloved pooch raises levels of oxytocin, the bonding hormone found in both dogs and humans. This helps each to understand the other's intentions and establishes a social connection. There is no denying their recognition of individual humans, as we frequently experience even when returning from a short period away from the house: we are greeted by fast-wagging tails and a high level of excitement in seeing our return. They know who keeps their dog bowls and tummies full.

A dog (or other pet) quickly becomes part of the family. Some of my friends who don't have children lavish all their love and attention on their fur babies. If you live alone, or have a partner who is a fly-in fly-out (FIFO) worker or frequently travels for work, a pet provides companionship and reassurance. All that unconditional love and affection that comes from having a dog or pet helps to fend off loneliness.

My friends fall into two groups: those who own dogs and those who don't. My non-dog-owning friends clearly think we're a bit bonkers and can't comprehend why we put up with all the terrible farts, dog breath, over-exuberant jumping and having to pick up mountains of dog poo. It's because we love them, and we believe they love us. But there's more to it than that. The benefits of pets interacting with humans extend to better human health.

Interacting with your pet indoors or outside is good for your physical and mental well-being. Dog owners have lower blood pressure, healthier cholesterol levels and lower risk of heart disease. All those daily walks keep you fitter and healthier. Dog owners are also less stressed. Studies have shown that our stress (cortisol) levels fall in the presence of a dog during a stressful time. Patting your pet and having lots of cuddles helps to keep you calmer, more social, less lonely and appreciative of what you have. New research shows how interaction in specific dog-related activities, such as grooming, feeding and playing, can help to reduce symptoms of depression, stress and fatigue.

Have I convinced you yet?

Seeing my two hounds bouncing around, interacting with other dogs and playing when taking them for their daily constitutional puts a smile on my face as much as theirs. Invariably, there's the opportunity for a quick chat or hello with fellow dog owners. Bonus! Our doggie walks are enjoyed by all.

If you've been feeling a bit low or are worried about something, have you noticed how your dog senses this? They'll come up and give you a gentle nudge with a nose or a paw – or, if it's my two, come and sit on top of you.

Spending time in a hospital is never much fun, especially if you're dealing with a significant illness or have to undergo some unpleasant procedures. A couple of years ago, I visited the Ronald McDonald House in Nedlands, Perth, which provides a home-away-from-home environment for seriously ill children and their families. During that visit, the most important person I met was Gus, a beautiful black labrador who pads around the house in his current role as Director of Hugs and Pats, putting smiles on the kids' faces and loving all the pats and cuddles he can get. Gus is highly adept at raising the spirits of everyone who meets him, increasing oxytocin levels and fostering trust.

Pets in the office and the classroom

Why would taking your dog to work with you be a good thing?

Studies have shown that having a calm and relaxed pet with you at work helps you to stay calm too. They assist in keeping stress levels down along with your blood pressure, improving your heart health and productivity.

If you've ever worked in a place where pets were allowed, you may have noticed a higher level of staff morale, collaboration and overall happiness. As Dr John Molineux, Senior Lecturer in Human Resource Management at Deakin University, reminds us, 'You have many non-work aspects to your life. Owning a pet is one of those, and pet ownership has a strong social networking aspect and a sense of community'.

Finally, an article in the *Harvard Business Review* proposed that having an office pet policy can enhance the workplace environment and leverage collaborative activities. Could this be a competitive advantage?

Don't forget, it's International Take Your Dog to Work Day on 21 June.

More research is needed to demonstrate the effectiveness of pets in the classroom, but anecdotally there appears to be some benefit.

ADHD is a neurodevelopment disorder that affects 8% of the world's children. These children often have difficulty with paying attention or finishing tasks. They may have poor impulse control, be very fidgety, have poor sleep or find it difficult to plan. School can be a real challenge for them. One study showed that a group of children with ADHD who read to a therapy dog for 30 minutes once a week showed better focusing skills than a control group who read to a puppet that looked like a dog.

Animal-assisted therapy (AAT) is about using animals to assist humans in dealing with trauma, stress and mental health issues, and has been applied in the classroom environment. For children with autism, contact with small animals such as dogs, cats or guinea pigs, and larger animals such as horses, has been shown to help the children emotionally and socially, boosting self-confidence and positive mood, and reducing behavioural problems. It's not a cure, but it does appear to help alleviate some of the symptoms associated with neurodiversity in children.

Equine therapy

Learning to ride a horse is not only great fun, it's also excellent for improving posture and balance, and building confidence, as well as getting you into nature.

Horse riding has been available as an activity for children and adults with disabilities for many years. Equine therapy is also used to assist individuals recovering from anxiety, post-traumatic stress disorder (PTSD) or chronic stress. Here, the equine therapist or mental health professional works with a client to build a trust-based relationship with the therapist horse before engaging in other activities like grooming, feeding or leading the animal under supervision. Because all the interaction is outside, it provides a non-threatening and calming environment. Horses are watchful and sensitive to movement and emotion, often mirroring a person's behaviour or emotion; this makes the human feel safe, understood and connected to the horse.

Horses are also used to teach leadership skills. In this context, business leaders learn the gentle art of 'followship' to improve their interpersonal communication skills, improve teamwork and bring about effective behavioural change in others.

Horses are herd animals and highly social. Their emotional intelligence and verbal and nonverbal communication sensitivity appear far more highly developed than humans'. A horse will always give you honest and immediate feedback on your behaviour!

In a nutshell

- Chapter 2 established that hearing birdsong can boost mental health and well-being, but other animals can also help improve your health.
- Wildlife interactions in our urban environments can provide mental, physical, social and spiritual benefits.
- Pets can improve both your mental health (boosting compassion and kindness towards others but also self-care) and physical health (by improving the health of your microbiome and making your immune function more robust, as well as raising levels of immunoglobulin A, which protects you from pathogens).
- Equine therapy has been shown to be effective in treating anxiety, PTSD and chronic stress.

Conclusion

Your nature prescription

Now that you've come to the end of this book, what will you do to reduce the impact of your stress on your health and happiness? This is where taking a look at what to include in your own nature prescription can be helpful so you can devise a simple framework to enable you to get outside more often.

Knowing what you want

Time in nature might feel unattainable, a luxury you can't currently afford, even though you know how much better you feel after a stroll in the park, a picnic by the river or time at the beach. But what if you could attain it?

What does health and well-being in nature look like to you? Would some of the benefits you might enjoy include:

- a greater sense of calm and inner peace
- feeling happy
- feeling healthier
- feeling energised, focused and attentive
- feeling less stressed
- feeling more connected and more self-aware?

Suppose you're aware of the gaps between where you are and where you want to be. How can you add some small changes to your daily schedule that will enable you to spend more time outside each day without it feeling like a chore or a burden in your already overburdened schedule?

A nature prescription is as it sounds: just like when you've been prescribed antibiotics, you need to know the dosage, frequency and duration. It's important to consider accessibility, how long you intend to spend in the activity, how often you can go and what level of intensity this activity will involve.

How much time is feasible to give? Your answer will depend on various factors:

- Do you work from home (and thus have less reason to leave the house)?
- Do you drive to and from your place of work, leaving your car in an underground or covered car park?
- Does your work require you to spend time outside (not just sitting in a vehicle)?
- Do you have a second job – taking care of your family and partner, supervising homework, ferrying the kids to various out-of-school activities, and doing the laundry, shopping and cleaning – that takes up all your 'spare' time?

If you've seen the statistics, you'll know that the vast majority of us spend 95% to 98% of our awake time indoors, which doesn't include 3% of our time spent in a vehicle. Can you start with five to ten minutes more time in nature a day?

The current minimum recommendation for time in nature to maintain your mental well-being is 120 minutes a week. More is better. Balancing this against the current recommendation for physical activity, which is 150 minutes of moderate physical activity a week plus two sessions of 30 minutes spent doing weight training and resistance exercise, you can see there's a need to be doing something outside on most days, specifically for between 20 and 30 minutes in each session.

Timothy Beatley and Tanya Denckla-Cobb from the University of Virginia came up with the idea of the nature pyramid, a metaphor similar to that used for dietary guidelines. It provides a basic framework that reminds us of the benefits of incorporating time in nature into our lives on a daily, weekly, monthly and annual basis.

It's about becoming aware of what's on offer in your local neighbourhood and taking steps to taste nature more often. Dr Rachel Hopman, a Professor of Psychology at the University of Utah, has simplified this concept into what she calls the 20-5-3 rule. This entails:

- 20 minutes in a green space three times a week
- five hours in a semi-wild environment once a month
- three days off-grid once a year.

Does this look doable to you? Remember, the numbers for time spent in nature are a guide only; they are not set in stone.

Setting yourself a goal provides direction and a sense of purpose, and achieving your goal is enormously rewarding. You feel good, you can't wipe the smile off your face, and you get lots of congratulatory pats on the back from friends and family. Bravo!

Your brain is delighted with your success. That sense of reward triggers the release of the neurochemical dopamine, making you feel good and motivating you to want to repeat that rewarding behaviour – meaning you set yourself another goal and go about achieving that.

But why wait for that end-of-project celebratory party? While having the biggest dopamine five-tiered cake in your favourite flavour will taste delicious, how much more delicious would it be to regularly enjoy that same cake as a bite-sized cupcake? This is where the nature pyramid can help. Now, you get to experience the five-tiered cake of reward every so often along with lots of smaller cupcakes along the way.

More dopamine more often. That's what your brain craves.

Your nature prescription

Let's look at what your weekly, monthly and annual dose of time in nature could look like.

Your weekly dose

The 20-5-3 rule stipulates 20 minutes in a green or blue space three times a week. That's just one hour. The issue I have with this is it's not long enough. So, let's break down this rule a bit further and look at what you can do daily to get out into the great outdoors and start to reap the benefits of lower stress, lower blood pressure and better mood.

If we are being pedantic, 120 minutes divided across seven days is 17 minutes and a few seconds. Let's round it up to 20 to 30 minutes. Here are the questions to ask yourself:

- **Do I have 20 minutes each day to get outside?** If your answer is no, then we have a problem that may boil down to priorities, or not believing enough in the value nature provides your health.

- **Where can I go for my 20 minutes outside?** This comes down to being aware of what's available in your neighbourhood. Do you know where your nearest parks, bushland or trail walks are? Do you know the easiest way to get to these? Is there a bus route? Is there parking, if you have to drive? The mantra is to find less concrete and more greenery.

- **When can I go?** If early morning is too chaotic, what about lunchtime? And no, the excuse of 'I don't stop for lunch' won't wash here. Taking 20 minutes for a lunchtime walk is energising and sets you up for a much more focused and productive afternoon, and it won't take long before you look forward to this time.

- **What will I do?** Ideally, this would involve walking, but sitting in nature is fine too if you've got a favourite spot. The main thing is to cancel all other distractions, such as your phone. This is not the time to make phone calls, listen to music or podcasts, or check your emails.

- **What if it's raining, 45 degrees Celsius or 40 degrees below?** Not every day is going to be a perfect day for being outside, so use your discretion. Can you change the time or location for your time outside to find greater shelter? Can you go for a longer duration on a different day?

Remember, this is about creating a habit of spending regular time in nature.

Also, look to mix it up. Is there an outdoor event you could get to? What about scheduling a regular walk with family or friends, choosing different locations to keep it interesting?

Notice what type of place suits you the best. Is it 20 minutes spent in your garden, or a lunchtime walk, or taking your kids to the local playground in the park, or picking some homegrown herbs or vegetables for dinner?

Your monthly dose

From small beginnings, now you can ramp up your nature engagement with a five-hour monthly immersion. This is about looking at how you can get out for a half-day or longer. Do you have a national park within reasonable driving or public transport distance? If you're not far from the coast, how about a day trip to the seaside or a fishing trip?

These times are best scheduled to make them happen. All you need is your calendar to mark your monthly trips. Invite some friends or make it a family excursion.

Again, the idea is to separate yourself from urban intrusions. Turn your phone to silent, and only use it to take pictures.

Sign up to learn new skills like kayaking, golf, beach volleyball or rock climbing! Maybe go for an overnight camp.

Your annual dose

This is where you can let your imagination go wild – within your budget, of course!

Since my husband and I started going off-grid on regular holidays, we knew there would be no turning back. The beauty for us is that it's easy to find those places we love within a reasonable drive time.

Depending on your preferences, your annual dose might be taken in a caravan, camper van or car. Do you prefer a tent, a boat, or a real bed and someone else cooking your evening meal?

Three days is the minimum here. It can take that long for your brain to uncouple itself from all those incessant worries and work-related thoughts. There is something deliciously liberating about not being able to access wi-fi or the Internet. No one can contact me – yippee!

Yes, nomophobia can be painful – that's the phantom pain associated with finding your phone is no longer connected to anything anymore. However, the gains are all positive. You start noticing more around you. You feel more relaxed. You sleep better (and often for longer), and you get this ridiculously big smile stuck on your face. You're happier, healthier and feeling great – it doesn't get better than that!

My caveat here is to be accessible somehow – via satellite phone or emergency position-indicating radio beacon (EPIRB), for example. Tell someone where you're going and when you expect to be back, and give them some emergency contacts. Travel with others and take spares of everything, including extra food and water.

#onesmallthing

Here we are at the end of the book. In reality, this is just the beginning of your journey towards better health, happiness and well-being.

The book was written as a reminder that each of us has the power to contribute to this. It's as simple as choosing to slow down, press pause and step outside. You now have the natural advantage of knowing that you can address some of the stresses and strains of everyday life by establishing small access points to nature.

A medical colleague recently commented to me that short GP consults or attending the emergency department for issues of loneliness or mental distress are inappropriate. But if a health practitioner doesn't have the time or capacity to deal with human suffering, where can an individual find help? Well, now you know.

This isn't to say that spending time in nature is the panacea to all our ills, nor should we avoid assistance from healthcare providers when warranted. However, the research is clear: green or social prescriptions provide a powerful adjunct for recovering from and preventing illness.

Small beginnings lead to bigger impacts. You could buy a green friend for that solitary fern looking a little lonesome and sad in the bathroom, schedule a short walk outside at lunchtime or watch more sunsets.

What #onesmallthing will you do to boost your natural advantage?

About the author

Jenny Brockis is ever curious to discover what empowers us to find greater happiness and better health and well-being.

As an experienced medical practitioner and board-certified Lifestyle Medicine Practitioner, Jenny understands the challenges of changing habits and thinking. Her unwavering commitment is to enlighten people about the factors that contribute to well-being, backed by solid scientific evidence.

Ever the optimist, she believes we can adapt and thrive in our rapidly changing world by nurturing our mind-body-nature connection.

She is the founder and director of consultancy Brain Fit and the bestselling author of *Future Brain* (Wiley), which was released in a second edition as *Smarter, Sharper Thinking*, and *Thriving Mind* (Wiley).

To learn more about her work, visit drjennybrockis.com.

References

A Prescription for Nature (PaRx), accessed 30 July 2024, parkprescriptions.ca.

Abbaspoor Z et al., 'The effect of citrus aurantium aroma on the sleep quality in postmenopausal women: a randomized controlled trial', *International Journal of Community Based Nursing and Midwifery*, vol. 10, no. 2, April 2022, pp. 86–95.

Abdolghanizadeh, S et al., 'Microbiota insights into pet ownership and human health', *Research in Veterinary Science*, vol. 171, May 2024, 105220.

Adam D, 'Chemical released by trees can help cool planet, scientists find', *The Guardian*, 1 November 2008, theguardian.com/environment/2008/oct/31/forests-climatechange.

Alcock I et al., 'Longitudinal effects on mental health of moving to greener and less green urban areas', *Environmental Science & Technology*, vol. 48, no. 2, 21 January 2014, pp. 1247–1255.

Allen S, *The Science of Awe*, report, Greater Good Science Center, September 2018, ggsc.berkeley.edu/images/uploads/GGSC-JTF_White_Paper-Awe_FINAL.pdf.

Andersen L, Corazon SS & Stigsdotter UK, 'Nature exposure and its effects on immune system functioning: a systematic review', *International Journal of Environmental Research and Public Health*, vol. 18, no. 4, 3 February 2021, 1416.

Ang C-S & MacDougall FA, 'An evaluation of animal-assisted therapy for autism spectrum disorders: therapist and parent perspectives', *Psychological Studies (Mysore)*, vol. 67, no. 1, 10 March 2022, pp. 72–81.

Atchley RA, Strayer DL & Atchley P, 'Creativity in the wild: improving creative reasoning through immersion in natural settings', *PLOS ONE*, vol. 7, no. 12, 12 December 2012, e51474.

Australian Academy of Health & Medical Sciences, *The Australian Bushfires: Impacts on health – the evidence*, report, 2020, aahms.org/wp-content/uploads/2022/02/The-Australian-Bushfires-and-the-impact-on-health_evidence-doc.pdf.

Australian Bureau of Statistics, 'National Study of Mental Health and Wellbeing', 2020-2022, abs.gov.au/statistics/health/mental-health/national-study-mental-health-and-wellbeing/2020-2022.

Australian Government Department of Health and Aged Care, 'Physical activity and exercise guidelines for all Australians', updated 7 May 2021, health.gov.au/topics/physical-activity-and-exercise/physical-activity-and-exercise-guidelines-for-all-australians/.

References

Azad MB et al., 'Infant gut microbiota and the hygiene hypothesis of allergic disease: impact of household pets and siblings on microbiota composition and diversity', *Allergy, Asthma, and Clinical Immunology: Official journal of the Canadian Society of Allergy and Clinical Immunology*, vol. 9, no. 1, 22 April 2013, 15.

Balanzá-Martínez V & Cervera-Martínez J, 'Lifestyle prescription for depression with a focus on nature exposure and screen time: a narrative review', *International Journal of Environmental Research and Public Health*, vol. 19, no. 9, 22 April 2022, 5094.

Basner M, 'Why Noise is Bad for your Health – and what you can do about it', video, TEDMED, 2018, tedmed.com/talks/show?id=730074.

Bates AE et al., 'Global COVID-19 lockdown highlights humans as both threats and custodians of the environment', *Biological Conservation*, vol. 263, November 2021, 109175.

Bauer A & White ND, 'Time in nature: a prescription for the prevention or management of hypertension', *American Journal of Lifestyle Medicine*, vol. 17, no. 4, 25 March 2023.

Beatley T, 'Exploring the nature pyramid', *The Nature of Cities*, 7 August 2012, thenatureofcities.com/2012/08/07/exploring-the-nature-pyramid/.

Benedyk A et al., 'Real-life behavioral and neural circuit markers of physical activity as a compensatory mechanism for social isolation', *Nature Mental Health*, vol. 2, 19 February 2024, pp. 337–342.

Bentley PR et al., 'Nature, smells, and human wellbeing', *Ambio*, vol. 52, 18 July 2022, pp. 1–14.

Berk M, Leboyer M & Sommer IE, *Immuno-Psychiatry: Facts and prospects*, Springer, 2021.

Berkman LF et al., 'From social integration to health: Durkheim in the new millennium', *Social Science & Medicine*, vol. 51, no. 6, 15 September 2000, pp. 843–857.

Berman MG, Jonides J & Kaplan S, 'The cognitive benefits of interacting with nature', *Psychological Science*, vol. 19, no. 12, December 2008, pp. 1207–1212.

Bernardi L, Porta C & Sleight P, 'Cardiovascular, cerebrovascular, and respiratory changes induced by different types of music in musicians and non-musicians: the importance of silence', *Heart* (British Cardiac Society); vol. 92, no. 4, April 2006, pp. 445–452.

Biofilico, 'Best examples of biophilic design office: sustainable interior – biofilico wellness interiors', accessed 30 July 2024, biofilico.com/news/5-best-examples-sustainable-office-interior-biophilic-design.

Bloomfield D, 'What makes nature-based interventions for mental health successful?' *BJPsych International*, vol. 14, no. 4, 2017, pp. 82–85.

Bloomfield SF et al., 'Too clean, or not too clean: the hygiene hypothesis and home hygiene', *Clinical and Experimental Allergy: Journal of the British Society for Allergy and Clinical Immunology*, vol. 36, no. 4, April 2006, pp. 402–425.

Böbel TS et al., 'Less immune activation following social stress in rural vs. urban participants raised with regular or no animal contact, respectively', *Proceedings of the National Academy of Sciences*, vol. 115, no. 20, 30 April 2018; pp. 5259–5264.

Borchers Arriagada N et al., 'Unprecedented smoke-related health burden associated with the 2019–20 bushfires in eastern Australia', *Medical Journal of Australia*, vol. 213, no. 6, 12 March 2020, pp. 282–283.

Boucher O et al., 'Clouds and aerosols', in Stocker TF et al. (eds), *Climate Change 2013: The Physical Science Basis. Contribution of Working Group I to the Fifth Assessment Report of the Intergovernmental Panel on Climate Change*, Cambridge University Press, 2018.

Bragg R et al., *Wellbeing Benefits from Natural Environments Rich in Wildlife: A literature review for The Wildlife Trusts*, University of Essex, September 2015, wildlifetrusts.org/sites/default/files/2018-05/r1_literature_review_wellbeing_benefits_of_wild_places_lres_0.pdf.

Bratman GN et al., 'The benefits of nature experience: improved affect and cognition', *Landscape and Urban Planning*, vol. 138, March 2015, pp. 41–50.

Bray EE et al., 'Early-emerging and highly heritable sensitivity to human communication in dogs', *Current Biology*, vol. 31, no. 14, 26 July 2021, pp. 3132–3136.

Brielmann AA et al., 'What happens in your brain when you walk down the street? Implications of architectural proportions, biophilia, and fractal geometry for urban science', *Urban Science*, vol. 6, no. 1, 7 January 2022, 3.

Britton E et al., 'Blue care: a systematic review of blue space interventions for health and wellbeing', *Health Promotion International*, vol. 35, no. 1, February 2020, pp. 50–69.

Burns AC et al., 'Day and night light exposure are associated with psychiatric disorders: an objective light study in >85,000 people', *Nature Mental Health*, vol. 1, 9 October 2023, pp. 853–862.

Burns AC et al., 'Time spent in outdoor light is associated with mood, sleep, and circadian rhythm-related outcomes: a cross-sectional and longitudinal study in over 400,000 UK Biobank participants', *Journal of Affective Disorders*, vol. 295, 1 December 2021, pp. 347–352.

Bushdid C et al., 'Humans can discriminate more than 1 trillion olfactory stimuli', *Science*, vol. 343, no. 6177, 21 March 2014, pp. 1370–1372.

Buxton RT et al., 'A synthesis of health benefits of natural sounds and their distribution in national parks', vol. 118, no. 4, 6 April 2021, e2013097118.

References

Calarco M, *Beating Burnout, Finding Balance: Mindful lessons for a meaningful life*, Wiley, 2023.

Campbell PD, Miller AM & Woesner ME, 'Bright light therapy: seasonal affective disorder and beyond', *The Einstein Journal of Biology and Medicine*, vol. 32, 2017, e13–e25.

Cao K et al., 'Significance of outdoor time for myopia prevention: a systematic review and meta-analysis based on randomized controlled trials', *Ophthalmic Research*, vol. 63, no. 2, March 2020, pp. 97–105.

Casey E et al., 'Association between fine particulate matter exposure and cerebrospinal fluid biomarkers of Alzheimer's disease among a cognitively healthy population-based cohort', *Environmental Health Perspectives*, vol. 132, no. 4, 3 April 2024, 047001.

Chang C et al., 'A lower connection to nature is related to lower mental health benefits from nature contact', *Scientific Reports*, vol. 14, 20 March 2024, 6705.

Chang SJ et al., 'Animal-assisted therapy as an intervention for older adults: a systematic review and meta-analysis to guide evidence-based practice', *Worldviews on Evidence-based Nursing*, vol. 18, no. 1, February 2021, pp. 60–67.

Charnetski CJ, Riggers S & Brennan FX, 'Effect of petting a dog on immune system function', *Psychological Reports*, vol. 95, no. 3 part 2, December 2004, pp. 1087–1091.

Chawla L, 'Childhood nature connection and constructive hope: a review of research on connecting with nature and coping with environmental loss', *People and Nature*, vol. 2, no. 3, September 2020, pp. 619–642.

Chirico A & Yaden DB, 'Awe: a self-transcendent and sometimes transformative emotion', in Lench HC (ed.), *The Function of Emotions: When and why emotions help us*, Springer, April 2018, pp. 221–233.

Christensen T, 'For green spaces to be most beneficial to health, they need to be walkable', *American Heart Association*, 30 November 2023, heart.org/en/news/2023/11/30/for-green-spaces-to-be-most-beneficial-to-health-they-need-to-be-walkable.

Cole SW et al., 'Myeloid differentiation architecture of leukocyte transcriptome dynamics in perceived social isolation', *Proceedings of the National Academy of Sciences*, vol. 112, no. 49, 8 December 2015, pp. 15142–15147.

Correia RA, 'Acknowledging and understanding the contributions of nature to human sense of time', *People and Nature*, vol. 6, no. 2, 5 March 2024, pp. 358–366.

Coutts C & Hahn M, 'Green infrastructure, ecosystem services, and human health', *International Journal of Environmental Research and Public Health*, vol. 12, no. 8, 18 August 2015, pp. 9768–9798.

Cyril Kurupp AR et al., 'The impact of the COVID-19 pandemic on myopia progression in children: a systematic review', *Cureus*, vol. 14, no. 8, 26 August 2022, e28444.

Dankiw KA et al., 'The impacts of unstructured nature play on health in early childhood development: a systematic review', *PLOS ONE*, vol. 15, no. 2, 13 February 2020, e0229006.

De Young R, 'Environmental psychology', in Alexander DE & Fairbridge RW (eds), *Encyclopedia of Environmental Science*, Kluwer Academic Publishers, 1999, pp. 223–224.

Deng L & Pang Y, 'Effect of outdoor activities in myopia control: meta-analysis of clinical studies', *Optometry and Vision Science: Official publication of the American Academy of Optometry*, vol. 96, no. 4, April 2019, pp. 276–282.

Diego MA & Field T, 'Moderate pressure massage elicits a parasympathetic nervous system response', *The International Journal of Neuroscience*, vol. 119, no. 5, 2009, pp. 630–638.

Djernis D et al., 'A systematic review and meta-analysis of nature-based mindfulness: effects of moving mindfulness training into an outdoor natural setting', *International Journal of Environmental Research and Public Health*, vol. 16, no. 17, 2 September 2019, 3202.

Ending Loneliness Together, accessed 30 July 2024, endingloneliness.com.au.

Engemann K et al., 'Residential green space in childhood is associated with lower risk of psychiatric disorders from adolescence into adulthood', *Biological Sciences*, vol. 116, no. 11, 14 January 2019, pp. 5188–5193.

Ephemeral New York, 'The baby cage craze never really caught on in New York City in the early 1900s', 18 December 023, ephemeralnewyork.wordpress.com/tag/luther-emmett-holt-airing-out-babies/.

Ettinger AK et al., 'Street trees provide an opportunity to mitigate urban heat and reduce risk of high heat exposure', *Scientific Reports*, vol. 14, 13 February 2024, 3266.

Ferraro DM, 'The phantom chorus: birdsong boosts human well-being in protected areas', *Proceedings of The Royal Society B: Biological Sciences*, vol. 287, no. 1941, 23 December 2020, 20201811.

Field RD et al., 'Inhaled water and salt suppress respiratory droplet generation and COVID-19 incidence and death on US coastlines', *Molecular Frontiers Journal*, vol. 5, no. 1, 2021, pp. 17–29.

Figueiro MG et al., 'The impact of daytime light exposures on sleep and mood in office workers', *Sleep Health*, vol. 3, no. 3, June 2017, pp. 204–215.

Flitcroft DI et al., 'IMI – defining and classifying myopia: a proposed set of standards for clinical and epidemiologic studies', *Investigative Ophthalmology & Visual Science*, vol. 6, no. 3, February 2019.

Foreman J et al., 'Association between digital smart device use and myopia: a systematic review and meta-analysis', *The Lancet Digital Health*, vol. 3, no. 12, December 2021, e806–e818.

References

Frank MG et al., 'Immunization with *Mycobacterium vaccae* induces an anti-inflammatory milieu in the CNS: attenuation of stress-induced microglial priming, alarmins and anxiety-like behavior', *Brain, Behavior, and Immunity*, vol. 73, October 2018, pp. 352–363.

GALLUP, *State of the Global Workplace: 2024 report*, report, 2024, gallup.com/workplace/349484/state-of-the-global-workplace.aspx.

Garrett JK et al., 'Coastal proximity and mental health among urban adults in England: the moderating effect of household income', *Health & Place*, vol. 59, September 2019, 102200.

Ge J et al., 'Local surface cooling from afforestation amplified by lower aerosol pollution', *Nature Geoscience*, vol. 16, 24 August 2023, pp. 781–788.

Georgiou M et al., 'Mechanisms of impact of blue spaces on human health: a systematic literature review and meta-analysis', *International Journal of Environmental Research and Public Health*. vol. 18, no. 5, 3 March 2021, 2486.

Goldy SP & Piff PK, 'Toward a social ecology of prosociality: why, when, and where nature enhances social connection', *Current Opinion in Psychology*, vol. 32, April 2020, pp. 27–31.

Gopalakrishnan V et al., 'Nature-based solutions can compete with technology for mitigating air emissions across the United States', *Environmental Science & Technology*, vol. 53, no. 22, 6 November 2019, pp. 13228–13237.

Gould van Praag CD et al., 'Mind-wandering and alterations to default mode network connectivity when listening to naturalistic versus artificial sounds', *Scientific Reports*, vol. 7, 27 March 2017, 45273.

Gray D et al., '(Re)connecting with nature: exploring nature-based interventions for psychological health and wellbeing', in Finneran N, Hewlett D & Clarke R (eds), *Managing Protected Areas*, Palgrave Macmillan, Cham, 27 December 2023.

Gray P, Lancy DF & Bjorklund DF, 'Decline in independent activity as a cause of decline in children's mental well-being: summary of the evidence', *The Journal of Pediatrics*, vol. 260, 2023, 113352.

Gupta S et al., 'Outdoor activity and myopia progression in children: a follow-up study using mixed-effects model', *Indian Journal of Ophthalmology*, vol. 69, no. 12, December 2021, pp. 3446–3450.

Guthold R et al., 'Global trends in insufficient physical activity among adolescents: a pooled analysis of 298 population-based surveys with 1·6 million participants', *The Lancet Child & Adolescent Health, vol. 4, no. 1, January 2020, pp. 23–35.

Ha S et al., 'Ambient air pollution and the risk of pregnancy loss: a prospective cohort study', *Fertility and Sterility*, vol. 109, no. 1, 16 November 2017, pp. 148–153.

Haahtela T, 'A biodiversity hypothesis', *Allergy*, vol. 74, no. 8, August 2019, pp. 1445–1456.

Haahtela T et al., 'A short history from Karelia study to biodiversity and public health interventions', *Frontiers in Allergy*, vol. 4, 14 March 2023.

Haidt J, *The Anxious Generation: How the great rewiring of childhood is causing an epidemic of mental illness*, Penguin Press, 2024.

Hajna S, Nafilyan V & Cummins S, 'Associations between residential greenspace exposure and mortality in 4 645 581 adults living in London, UK: a longitudinal study', *The Lancet Planetary Health*, vol. 7, no. 6, June 2023, e459–e468.

Hall K et al., *Using urban blue spaces to benefit population health and wellbeing*, report, Blue Health, 20 November 2020, zenodo.org/records/4277346.

Hammoud R et al., 'Lonely in a crowd: investigating the association between overcrowding and loneliness using smartphone technologies', *Scientific Reports*, vol. 11, no. 1, 20 December 2021, 24134.

Hammoud R et al., 'Smartphone-based ecological momentary assessment reveals mental health benefits of birdlife', *Scientific Reports*, vol. 12, 27 October 2022, 17589.

Harkness J, *Bird Therapy*, Unbound Digital, 13 June 2019.

Harrington SC, Stack J & O'Dwyer V, 'Risk factors associated with myopia in schoolchildren in Ireland', *The British Journal of Ophthalmology*, vol. 103, no. 12, December 2019, pp. 1803–1809.

Heart Foundation, 'Environment, climate change and heart health', accessed 1 August 2024, heartfoundation.org.au/heart-health-education/climate-change-and-heart-health.

Hedge A & Nou D, 'Worker reactions to electrochromic and low e glass office windows', *Ergonomics International Journal*, vol. 2, no. 4, 23 July 2018.

Heissel A et al., 'Exercise as medicine for depressive symptoms? A systematic review and meta-analysis with meta-regression', *British Journal of Sports Medicine*, vol. 57, no. 16, August 2023, pp. 1049–1057.

Holt LE, *The Care and Feeding of Children*, D. Appleton and Company, 1900.

Holt-Lunstad J et al., 'Loneliness and social isolation as risk factors for mortality: a meta-analytic review', *Perspectives on Psychological Science*, vol. 10, no. 2, 11 March 2015, pp. 227–237.

Hopman-Droste R et al., 'How nature helps replenish our depleted cognitive reserves and improves mood by increasing activation of the brain's default mode network', in Lane SM & Atchley P (eds), *Human Capacity in the Attention Economy*, American Psychological Association, September 2020, pp. 159–187.

Howe R et al., 'Animal assisted interventions in the children's hospital: protocol for a scoping review', *HRB Open Research*, vol. 3, no. 74, 14 May 2021.

Hsieh C-H et al., 'The effect of water sound level in virtual reality: a study of restorative benefits in young adults through immersive natural environments', *Journal of Environmental Psychology*, vol. 88, June 2023, 102012.

Hunter MR, Gillespie BW & Chen SY-P, 'Urban nature experiences reduce stress in the context of daily life based on salivary biomarkers', *Frontiers in Psychology*, vol. 10, no. 722, 4 April 2019.

References

Ideno Y, 'Blood pressure-lowering effect of *Shinrin-yoku* (forest bathing): a systematic review and meta-analysis', *BMC Complementary and Alternative Medicine*, vol. 17, 16 August 2017, 409.

International Noise Awareness Day, 'Impact of noise on childhood cognitive development', accessed 30 July 2024, noiseawareness.org/info-center/classroom-acoustics/.

Ipsos, *World Mental Health Day 2023: A global advisor survey*, report, October 2023, ipsos.com/en/world-mental-health-day-2023.

Iungman T et al., 'Cooling cities through urban green infrastructure: a health impact assessment of European cities', *The Lancet*, vol. 401, no. 10376, 18 February 2023, pp. 577–589.

James JJ, Christiana RW & Battista RA, 'A historical and critical analysis of park prescriptions', *Journal of Leisure Research*, vol. 50, no. 4, pp. 311–329.

Jiang B, Schmillen R & Sullivan WC, 'How to waste a break: using portable electronic devices substantially counteracts attention enhancement effects of green spaces', *Environment and Behavior*, vol. 51, no. 9–10, 16 July 2018.

Jimenez MP et al., 'Associations between nature exposure and health: a review of the evidence', *International Journal of Environmental Research and Public Health*, vol. 18, no. 9, 30 April 2021, 4790.

Joshi A & Hinkley T, 'Too much time on screens? Screen time effects and guidelines for children and young people', Australian Institute of Family Studies, August 2021, aifs.gov.au/resources/short-articles/too-much-time-screens.

Kahriman Pamuk D & Ahi B, 'A phenomenological study on the school concept of the children attending the forest school', *Journal of Qualitative Research in Education*, vol. 7, no. 4, 24 October 2019.

Kates AE et al., 'Household pet ownership and the microbial diversity of the human gut microbiota', *Frontiers in Cellular and Infection Microbiology*, vol. 10, no. 73, 28 February 2020.

Katz DL et al., 'Lifestyle as medicine: the case for a true health initiative', *American Journal of Health Promotion*, vol. 32, no. 6, July 2018, pp. 1452–1458.

Keller J et al., 'Forest bathing increases adolescents' mental well-being: a mixed-methods study', *International Journal of Environmental Research and Public Health*, vol. 21, no. 1, 2024, 8.

Kelly J & Bird E, 'Improved mood following a single immersion in cold water', *Lifestyle Medicine*, vol. 3, no. 1, 2 December 2021, e53.

Keltner D & Haidt J, 'Approaching awe, a moral, spiritual, and aesthetic emotion', *Cognition and Emotion*, vol. 17, no. 2, 18 August 2010, pp. 297–314.

Kirste I et al., 'Is silence golden? Effects of auditory stimuli and their absence on adult hippocampal neurogenesis', *Brain Structure & Function*, vol. 220, no. 2, March 2015, pp. 1221–1228.

Klepeis NE et al., 'The National Human Activity Pattern Survey (NHAPS): a resource for assessing exposure to environmental pollutants', *Journal of Exposure Science & Environmental Epidemiology*, vol. 11, 26 July 2001, pp. 231–252.

Knechtle B et al., 'Cold water swimming – benefits and risks: a narrative review', *International Journal of Environmental Research and Public Health*, vol. 17, no. 23, 2 December 2020, 8984.

Knight T et al., 'How effective is "greening" of urban areas in reducing human exposure to ground-level ozone concentrations, UV exposure and the "urban heat island effect"? An updated systematic review', *Environmental Evidence*, vol. 10, 5 June 2021, 12.

Knobler SL et al. (eds), 'The threat of pandemic influenza: are we ready? Workshop summary', *The National Academies Collection: Reports funded by National Institutes of Health*, National Academies Press (U.S.), 2005.

Ko L-W et al., 'A pilot study on essential oil aroma stimulation for enhancing slow-wave EEG in sleeping brain', *Scientific Reports*, vol. 11, 13 January 2021, 1078.

Kondola A et al., 'Depressive symptoms and objectively measured physical activity and sedentary behaviour throughout adolescence: a prospective cohort study', *The Lancet Psychiatry*, vol. 7, no. 3, March 2020, pp. 262–271.

Konijnendijk C, 'The 3-30-300 rule for urban forestry and greener cities', *Biophilic Cities Journal*, vol. 4, no. 2, July 2021.

Kotera Y, Richardson M & Sheffeld D, 'Effects of shinrin-yoku (forest bathing) and nature therapy on mental health: a systematic review and meta-analysis', *International Journal of Mental Health and Addiction*, vol. 20, 28 July 2020, pp. 337–361.

Kraus N, *Of Sound Mind: How our brain constructs a meaningful sonic world*, MIT Press, 27 September 2022.

Kuo M, 'How might contact with nature promote human health? Promising mechanisms and a possible central pathway', *Frontiers in Psychology*, vol. 6, 25 August 2015.

Kuo M, Browning MHEM & Penner ML, 'Do lessons in nature boost subsequent classroom engagement? Refuelling students in flight' *Frontiers in Psychology*, vol. 8, 4 January 2018.

Landreneau JR, Hesemann NP & Cardonell MA, 'Review on the myopia pandemic: epidemiology, risk factors, and prevention', *Missouri Medicine*, vol. 118, no. 2, March–April 2021, pp. 156–163.

Landrigan PJ et al., 'The *Lancet* commission on pollution and health', *The Lancet*, vol. 391, no. 10119, 3 February 2018, pp. 462–512.

Larouche R et al., 'Determinants of outdoor time in children and youth: a systematic review of longitudinal and intervention studies', *International Journal of Environmental Research and Public Health*. vol. 20, no. 2, 11 January 2023, 1328.

References

Lass-Hennemann J et al., 'Presence of a dog reduces subjective but not physiological stress responses to an analog trauma', *Frontiers in Psychology*, vol. 5, 9 September 2014.

Leach J, *Happiness grows on trees: how woodlands boost our wellbeing*, Woodlands.co.uk, February 2013, woodlands.co.uk/Woodlands.co.uk-HappinessGrowsOnTrees-Feb13.pdf.

Lee J-Y et al., 'Diving bradycardia of elderly Korean women divers, haenyeo, in cold seawater: a field report', *Industrial Health*, vol. 54, no. 2, 2016, pp. 183–190.

Li Q, 'Effects of forest environment (Shinrin-yoku/Forest bathing) on health promotion and disease prevention – the Establishment of "Forest Medicine"', *Environmental Health and Preventive Medicine*, vol. 27, no. 43, 2022.

Li Q, *Forest Bathing: How trees can help you find health and happiness*, Penguin Publishing Group, 2018.

Li Q et al., 'A day trip to a forest park increases human natural killer activity and the expression of anti-cancer proteins in male subjects', *Journal of Biological Regulators and Homeostatic Agents*, vol. 24, no. 2, April–June 2010, pp. 157–165.

Li Q et al., 'Effects of forest bathing (shinrin-yoku) on serotonin in serum, depressive symptoms and subjective sleep quality in middle-aged males', *Environmental Health and Preventive Medicine*, vol. 27, no. 44, 2022.

Lieberman MD, *Social: Why our brains are wired to connect*, Crown Publishing Group, 2013.

Lingham G et al., 'How does spending time outdoors protect against myopia? A review', *The British Journal of Ophthalmology*, vol. 104, no. 5, November 2019, 314675.

Lødrup Carlsen KC et al., 'Does pet ownership in infancy lead to asthma or allergy at school age? Pooled analysis of individual participant data from 11 European birth cohorts', *PLOS ONE*, vol. 7, no. 8, 29 August 2012, e43214.

Loudon ASI, 'Circadian biology: a 2.5 billion year old clock', *Current Biology*, vol. 22, no. 14, 24 July 2012, R570–R571.

Louv R, *Last Child in the Woods: Saving our children from nature-deficit disorder*, Algonquin Books, 2008.

MacKerron G & Mourato S, 'Happiness is greater in natural environments', *Global Environmental Change*, vol. 23, no. 5, 20 May 2013, pp. 992–1000.

Makram OM et al., 'Nature and mental health in urban Texas: a NatureScore-based study', *International Journal of Environmental Research and Public Health*, vol. 21, no. 2, 1 February 2024, 168.

Malcolm M, Frost H & Cowie J, 'Loneliness and social isolation causal association with health-related lifestyle risk in older adults: a systematic review and meta-analysis protocol', *Systematic Reviews*, vol. 8, 2019, 48.

Manolis AS et al., 'Winter swimming: body hardening and cardiorespiratory protection via sustainable acclimation', *Current Sports Medicine Reports*, vol. 18, no. 11, November 2019, pp. 401–415.

Maranda L et al., 'A novel behavioral intervention in adolescents with type 1 diabetes mellitus improves glycemic control: preliminary results from a pilot randomized control trial', *The Science of Diabetes Self-Management and Care*, vol. 41, no. 2, 22 January 2015.

Mariotti A, 'The effects of chronic stress on health: new insights into the molecular mechanisms of brain–body communication', *Future Science OA*, vol. 1, no. 3, 17 June 2015.

McCarthy M, Mynott J & Marren P, *The Consolation of Nature: Spring in the time of Coronavirus*, Hodder & Stoughton, 2020.

McDonnell AS & Strayer DL, 'Immersion in nature enhances neural indices of executive attention', *Scientific Reports*, vol. 14, no. 1845, 22 January 2024.

McGrath JJ et al., 'Age of onset and cumulative risk of mental disorders: a cross-national analysis of population surveys from 29 countries', *The Lancet Psychiatry*, vol. 10, no. 9, September 2023, pp. 668–681.

McPherson G et al., 'Municipal forest benefits and costs in five US cities', *Journal of Forestry*, vol. 103, no. 8, December 2005, pp. 411–416.

Mead MN, 'Benefits of sunlight: a bright spot for human health', *Environmental Health Perspectives*, vol. 116, no. 4, April 2008 A160–A167.

Meister, J, *The Employee Experience: Study: employees desire natural light and views over any other office perk*, report, Future Workplace, n.d., view.com/sites/default/files/documents/Future-Workplace-The-Employee-Experience.pdf.

Meredith GR et al., 'Minimum time dose in nature to positively impact the mental health of college-aged students, and how to measure it: a scoping review'. *Frontiers in Psychology*, vol. 10, 14 January 2020; 2942.

Mills KT, Stefanescu A & He J, 'The global epidemiology of hypertension', *Nature Reviews Nephrology*, vol. 16, no. 4, April 2020, pp. 223–237.

Mirghafourvand M et al., 'Effect of orange peel essential oil on postpartum sleep quality: a randomized controlled clinical trial', *European Journal of Integrative Medicine*, vol. 8, no. 1, February 2016, pp. 62–66.

Moncrieff J et al., 'The serotonin theory of depression: a systematic umbrella review of the evidence', *Molecular Psychiatry*, vol. 28, 20 July 2022, pp. 3243–3256.

Monroe L, 'Horticulture therapy improves the body, mind and spirit', *Journal of Therapeutic Horticulture*, vol. 25, no. 2, 2015, pp. 33–40.

Moreno MA, Chassaikos YR & Cross C, 'Media use in school-aged children and adolescents', *Pediatrics*, vol. 138, no. 5, November 2016; e20162592.

Morgan IG, 'What public policies should be developed to deal with the epidemic of myopia?' *Optometry and Vision Science: Official publication of the American Academy of Optometry*, vol. 93, no. 9, September 2016, pp. 1058–1060.

References

Morsink K, 'With every breath you take, thank the ocean', *Smithsonian Ocean*, July 2017, ocean.si.edu/ocean-life/plankton/every-breath-you-take-thank-ocean.

Mure LS et al., 'Functional diversity of human intrinsically photosensitive retinal ganglion cells', *Science*, vol. 366, no. 6470, 6 December 2019, pp. 1251–1255.

Murrin E et al., 'Does physical activity mediate the associations between blue space and mental health? A cross-sectional study in Australia', *BMC Public Health*, vol. 23, 30 January 2023, 203.

Nagasawa M et al., Oxytocin-gaze positive loop and the coevolution of human-dog bonds', *Science*, vol. 348, no. 6232, 17 April 2015, pp. 333–336.

National Center for Cold Water Safety (U.S.), accessed 1 August 2024, coldwatersafety.org.

National Health Service (NHS) England, 'Green social prescribing', accessed 30 July 2024, england.nhs.uk/personalisedcare/social-prescribing/green-social-prescribing/.

National Park Service (U.S.), 'Sound gallery', updated 28 December 2022, nps.gov/subjects/sound/gallery.htm.

Nature Rx, accessed 2 August 2024, naturerx.cornell.edu/default.

Nejade RM, Grace D & Bowman LR, 'What is the impact of nature on human health? A scoping review of the literature', *Journal of Global Health*, vol. 12, no. 04099, 16 December 2022.

Nermes M et al., 'Furry pets modulate gut microbiota composition in infants at risk for allergic disease', *The Journal of Allergy and Clinical Immunology*, vol. 136, no. 6, December 2015, pp. 1688–1690.

Nguyen P-Y et al., 'Effect of nature prescriptions on cardiometabolic and mental health, and physical activity: a systematic review', *The Lancet Planetary Health*, vol. 7, no. 4, April 2023, e313–328.

Nichols WJ, *Blue Mind: The surprising science that shows how being near, in, on, or under water can make you happier, healthier, more connected, and better at what you do*, Back Bay Books, 2015.

Nikolaev YA et al., 'Lamellar cells in Pacinian and Meissner corpuscles are touch sensors', *Science Advances*, vol. 6, no. 51, 16 December 2020.

Noetel M et al., 'Effect of exercise for depression: systematic review and network meta-analysis of randomised controlled trials', *BMJ*, vol. 384, 2024, e075847.

Noseworthy M et al., 'The effects of outdoor versus indoor exercise on psychological health, physical health, and physical activity behaviour: a systematic review of longitudinal trials', *International Journal of Environmental Research and Public Health*, vol. 20, no. 3, 17 January 2023, 1669.

Nutsford D et al., 'Residential exposure to visible blue space (but not green space) associated with lower psychological distress in a capital city', *Health & Place*, vol. 39, May 2016, pp. 70–78.

O'Brien ME et al., 'A randomized phase II study of SRL172 (Mycobacterium vaccae) combined with chemotherapy in patients with advanced inoperable non-small-cell lung cancer and mesothelioma', *British Journal of Cancer*, vol. 83, no. 7, October 2000, pp. 853–857.

Olive R & Wheaton B, 'Understanding blue spaces: sport, bodies, wellbeing, and the sea', Moving Oceans, 25 August 2020, movingoceans.com/ocean-plastics/understanding-blue-spaces-sport-bodies-wellbeing-and-the-sea/.

Packheiser J et al., 'A systematic review and multivariate meta-analysis of the physical and mental health benefits of touch interventions', *Nature Human Behaviour*, vol. 8, no. 6, June 2024, pp. 1088–1107.

Pálsdóttir AM et al., 'Garden smellscape–experiences of plant scents in a nature-based intervention', *Frontiers in Psychology*, vol. 12, 29 June 2021.

Pasanen TP et al., 'Urban green space and mental health among people living alone: the mediating roles of relational and collective restoration in an 18-country sample', *Environmental Research*, vol. 232, 1 September 2023, 116324.

Pega F et al., 'Global, regional, and national burdens of ischemic heart disease and stroke attributable to exposure to long working hours for 194 countries, 2000–2016: A systematic analysis from the WHO/ILO Joint Estimates of the Work-related Burden of Disease and Injury', *Environment International*, vol. 154, September 2021, 106595.

Perl O et al., 'Odors enhance slow-wave activity in non-rapid eye movement sleep', Journal of Neurophysiology, vol. 115, no. 5, 1 May 2016, pp. 2294–2302.

Pijnenburg MW, Nantanda R, 'Rising and falling prevalence of asthma symptoms', *The Lancet*, vol. 398, no. 10311, 30 October 2021, pp. 1542–1543.

Porter J et al., 'Mechanisms of scent-tracking in humans', *Nature Neuroscience*, vol. 10, 1 February 2007, pp. 27–29.

Prisk C & Cusworth H, *From Muddy Hands and Dirty Faces... to Higher Grades and Happy Places: Outdoor learning and play at schools around the world*, report, Outdoor Classroom Day, November 2018, outdoorclassroomday.com/resource/muddy-hands-report/.

Prüss-Ustün A et al., 'Diseases due to unhealthy environments: an updated estimate of the global burden of disease attributable to environmental determinants of health', *Journal of Public Health* (Oxford, U.K.), vol. 39, no. 3, September 2017, pp. 464–475.

Quan SX & Schabram K, 'Research: the benefits of a pet-friendly workplace', *Harvard Business Review*, 13 November 2023, hbr.org/2023/11/research-the-benefits-of-a-pet-friendly-workplace.

Quan SX et al., 'All creatures great and small: a review and typology of employee-animal interactions', *Journal of Management*, vol. 50, no. 1, 17 August 2023, pp. 380–411.

References

Queiroz Almeida D et al., 'Green and blue spaces and lung function in the Generation XXI cohort: a life-course approach', *The European Respiratory Journal*, vol. 60, no. 6, 22 December 2022, 2103024.

Rahman MA et al., 'Traits of trees for cooling urban heat islands: a meta-analysis', *Building and Environment*, vol. 170, March 2020, 106606.

Raina MacIntyre C et al., 'Adverse health effects in people with and without preexisting respiratory conditions during bushfire smoke exposure in the 2019/2020 Australian summer', *American Journal of Respiratory and Critical Care*, vol. 204, no. 3, 11 May 2021.

Ramasubramanian A, 'Sunlight exposure reduces myopia in children', American Academy of Ophthalmology, 20 August 2018, aao.org/education/editors-choice/sunlight-exposure-reduces-myopia-in-children.

Razani N et al., 'Effect of park prescriptions with and without group visits to parks on stress reduction in low-income parents: SHINE randomized trial', *PLOS ONE*, vol. 13, no. 2, 2018, e0192921.

RECETAS, accessed 2 August 2024, recetasproject.eu.

Rideout V et al., *The Common Sense Census: Media use by tweens and teens, 2021*, report, 2022, commonsensemedia.org/sites/default/files/research/report/8-18-census-integrated-report-final-web_0.pdf.

Ritchie H, Samborska V & Roser M, 'Urbanization', Our World in Data, revised February 2024, ourworldindata.org/urbanization.

Robles KE et al. 'A shared fractal aesthetic across development', *Humanities and Social Sciences Communications*, vol. 7, no. 158, 25 November 2020.

Rodney RM et al., 'Physical and mental health effects of bushfire and smoke in the Australian Capital Territory 2019–20', *Frontiers in Public Health*, vol. 9, 14 October 2021, 682402.

Rosales Chavez J-B et al., 'Evaluating how varied human-wildlife interactions affect physical, mental, social, and spiritual health', *SSM - Qualitative Research in Health*, vol. 4, December 2023, 100302.

Rose KA et al., 'Outdoor activity reduces the prevalence of myopia in children', *Ophthalmology*, vol. 115, no. 8, August 2008, pp. 1279–1285.

Roslund MI et al., 'Biodiversity intervention enhances immune regulation and health-associated commensal microbiota among daycare children', *Science Advances*, vol. 6, no. 42, October 2020, eaba2578.

Rudd M, Vohs KD & Aaker J, 'Awe expands people's perception of time, alters decision making, and enhances well-being', *Psychological Science*, vol. 23, no. 10, 2012, pp. 1130–1136.

Ruokolainen L et al., 'Significant disparities in allergy prevalence and microbiota between the young people in Finnish and Russian Karelia', *Clinical & Experimental Allergy*, vol. 47, no. 5, 6 February 2017, pp. 665–674.

Ruppanner L et al., *2023 State of the Future of Work*, report, The University of Melbourne, March 2023, work-futures.org/publications.

Russo A & Andreucci MB, 'Raising healthy children: promoting the multiple benefits of green open spaces through biophilic design', *Sustainability*, vol. 15, no. 3, 20 January 2023, 1982.

Rutz C et al., 'COVID-19 lockdown allows researchers to quantify the effects of human activity on wildlife', *Nature Ecology & Evolution*, vol. 4, 2020, pp. 1156–1159.

Sabiniewicz A et al., 'Effects of odors on sleep quality in 139 healthy participants', *Scientific Reports*, vol. 12, 13 October 2022, 17165.

Sasso JM et al., 'Gut microbiome–brain alliance: a landscape view into mental and gastrointestinal health and disorders', *ACS Chemical Neuroscience*, vol. 14, no. 10, 8 May 2023, pp. 1717–1763.

Schredl M et al., 'Information processing during sleep: the effect of olfactory stimuli on dream content and dream emotions', *Journal of Sleep Research*, vol. 18, no. 3, September 2009, pp. 285–290.

Schuck SEB et al., 'Canine-assisted therapy for children with ADHD: preliminary findings from the positive assertive cooperative kids study', *Journal of Attention Disorders*, vol. 19, no. 2, February 2015, pp. 125–137.

See L, *The Island Of Sea Women*, Scribner, 2019.

Shanahan DF et al., 'Health benefits from nature experiences depend on dose', *Scientific Reports*, vol. 6, 23 June 2016, 28551.

Singh B et al., 'Effectiveness of physical activity interventions for improving depression, anxiety and distress: an overview of systematic reviews', *British Journal of Sports Medicine*, vol. 57, no. 18, September 2023, pp. 1203–1209.

Sleurs H et al., 'Exposure to residential green space and bone mineral density in young children', *JAMA Network Open*, vol. 7, no. 1, 2 January 2024, e2350214.

Smith B, 'The "pet effect" – health related aspects of companion animal ownership', *Australian Family Physician*, vol. 41, no. 6, June 2012, pp. 439–442.

Smith N et al., 'Urban blue spaces and human health: a systematic review and meta-analysis of quantitative studies', *Cities*, vol. 119, December 2021, 103413.

Song I et al., 'Effects of nature sounds on the attention and physiological and psychological relaxation', *Urban Forestry & Urban Greening*, vol. 86, August 2023, 127987.

Souter-Brown G, Hinckson E & Duncan S, 'Effects of a sensory garden on workplace wellbeing: a randomised control trial', *Landscape and Urban Planning*, vol. 207, March 2021, 103997.

Spahr-Emory R, 'Air pollution boosts Alzheimer's disease risk', *Futurity*, 11 April 2024, futurity.org/air-pollution-alzheimers-disease-risk-3205352/.

References

Spencer C & Gee K, 'Environmental psychology', in Smith PK & Hart CH (eds), *The Wiley Blackwell Handbook of Childhood Social Development*, 2nd edn, Wiley Blackwell, 2014, pp. 207–223.

Spencer C, Gee K & Sutton J, 'The roots and branches of environmental psychology', The British Psychological Society, 25 February 2009, bps.org.uk/psychologist/roots-and-branches-environmental-psychology.

Spracklen DV, Bonn B & Carslaw KS, 'Boreal forests, aerosols and the impacts on clouds and climate', *Philosophical Transactions: Series A, Mathematical, Physical and Engineering Sciences*, vol. 366, no. 1885, 28 December 2008, pp. 4613–4626.

Stellar JE et al., 'Awe and humility', *Journal of Personality and Social Psychology*, vol. 114, no. 2, February 2018, pp. 258–269.

Stenfors CUD et al., 'Positive effects of nature on cognitive performance across multiple experiments: test order but not affect modulates the cognitive effects', *Frontiers in Psychology*, vol. 10, no. 1413, 3 July 2019.

Stothard ER et al., 'Circadian entrainment to the natural light-dark cycle across seasons and the weekend', *Current Biology*, vol. 27, no. 4, 20 February 2017, pp. 508–513.

Strayer D, 'Restore your brain with nature', video, TEDxManhattanBeach, 13 December 2017, youtube.com/watch?v=_vRMRBxvtZA&t=134s.

Sudimac S, Sale V & Kühn S, 'How nature nurtures: amygdala activity decreases as the result of a one-hour walk in nature', *Molecular Psychiatry*, vol. 27, 5 September 2022, pp. 4446–4452.

Surma S, Oparil S & Narkiewicz K, 'Pet ownership and the risk of arterial hypertension and cardiovascular disease', *Current Hypertension Reports*, vol. 24, 22 April 2022, pp. 295–302.

Takeda M et al., 'Effects of bathing in different hot spring types on Japanese gut microbiota', *Scientific Reports*, vol. 14, 28 January 2024, 2316.

Takeda M et al., 'Hot spring bathing practices have a positive effect on mental health in Japan', *Heliyon*, vol. 9, no. 9, 29 August 2023, e19631.

Talens-Estarelles C et al., 'The effects of breaks on digital eye strain, dry eye and binocular vision: testing the 20-20-20 rule', *Contact Lens and Anterior Eye*, vol. 46, no. 2, April 2023, 101744.

Tang Y-Y, Hölzel BK & Posner MI, 'The neuroscience of mindfulness meditation', *Nature Reviews Neuroscience*, vol. 16, 18 March 2015, pp. 213–225.

Telethon Kids Institute, 'Vitamin D and sunlight', accessed 1 August 2024, telethonkids.org.au/our-research/research-topics/vitamin-d-and-sunlight/.

Thoreau HD, *Walden; or, Life in the Woods*, Ticknor and Fields, 1854.

Tiotiu AI et al., 'Impact of air pollution on asthma outcomes', *International Journal of Environmental Research and Public Health*, vol. 17, no. 17, 27 August 2020, 6212.

Tipton M, 'Cold water immersion: sudden death and prolonged survival', *The Lancet* (London, U.K.), vol 362, 2003, s12–13.

Trovato B et al., 'Physical activity, sun exposure, vitamin D intake and perceived stress in Italian adults', *Nutrients*, vol. 15, no. 10, 13 May 2023, 2301.

Tsui B, *Why We Swim*, Penguin Books, 2020.

Tsunetsugu Y, Park B-J & Miyazaki Y, 'Trends in research related to "Shinrin-yoku" (taking in the forest atmosphere or forest bathing) in Japan', *Environmental Health and Preventive Medicine*, vol. 15, 9 July 2009, pp. 27–37.

Tun HM et al., 'Exposure to household furry pets influences the gut microbiota of infant at 3–4 months following various birth scenarios', *Microbiome*, vol. 5, no. 1, 6 April 2017, 40.

Turunen AW et al., 'Cross-sectional associations of different types of nature exposure with psychotropic, antihypertensive and asthma medication', *Occupational and Environmental Medicine* vol. 80, no. 2, February 2023, pp. 111–118.

Twohig-Bennett C & Jones A, 'The health benefits of the great outdoors: a systematic review and meta-analysis of greenspace exposure and health outcomes', *Environmental Research*, vol. 166, October 2018, pp. 628–637.

Uetake J et al., 'Airborne bacteria confirm the pristine nature of the Southern Ocean boundary layer', *Proceedings of the National Academy of Sciences*, vol. 117, no. 24, 1 June 2020, pp. 13275–13282.

Ulrich RS, 'Natural versus urban scenes: some psychophysiological effects', *Environment and Behavior*, vol. 13, no. 5, September 1981.

Ulrich RS, 'View through a window may influence recovery from surgery', *Science* (New York, NY), vol. 27, no. 224 (4647), 27 April 1984, pp. 420–421.

Ulset V et al., 'Time spent outdoors during preschool: links with children's cognitive and behavioral development', *Journal of Environmental Psychology*, vol. 52, October 2017, pp. 69–80.

United Nations Department of Economic and Social Affairs, '68% of the world population projected to live in urban areas by 2050, says UN', 16 May 2018, un.org/development/desa/en/news/population/2018-revision-of-world-urbanization-prospects.html.

United States Environmental Protection Agency, 'Using trees and vegetation to reduce heat islands', accessed 1 August 2024, epa.gov/heatislands/using-trees-and-vegetation-reduce-heat-islands.

Van Leeuwen E et al., 'Approaches for discontinuation versus continuation of long-term antidepressant use for depressive and anxiety disorders in adults', *The Cochrane Database of Systematic Reviews*, vol. 4, no. 4, 15 April 2021, CD013495.

van Tulleken C et al., 'Open water swimming as a treatment for major depressive disorder', *BMJ Case Reports*, 21 August 2018, bcr2018225007.

References

Vert C et al., 'Physical and mental health effects of repeated short walks in a blue space environment: a randomised crossover study', *Environmental Research*, vol. 188, September 2020, 109812.

Wade DT & Halligan PW, 'The biopsychosocial model of illness: a model whose time has come', *Clinical Rehabilitation*, vol. 31, no. 8, 21 July 2017.

Wallisch P et al., 'The visible gorilla: Unexpected fast—not physically salient—objects are noticeable', *Proceedings of the National Academy of Sciences*, vol. 120, no. 22, 22 May 2023, e2214930120.

Wang H et al. 'Efficient removal of ultrafine particles from diesel exhaust by selected tree species: implications for roadside planting for improving the quality of urban air', *Environmental Science & Technology*, vol. 53, no. 12, 16 May 2019, pp. 6906–6916.

Wang Z et al., 'Global, regional, and national burden of asthma and its attributable risk factors from 1990 to 2019: a systematic analysis for the Global Burden of Disease Study 2019', *Respiratory Research*, vol. 24, 23 June 2023, 169.

Warembourg C et al., 'Urban environment during early-life and blood pressure in young children', *Environment International*, vol. 146, January 2021, 106174.

Weinstein N et al., 'Balance between solitude and socializing: everyday solitude time both benefits and harms well-being', *Scientific Reports*, vol. 13, 2023, 21160.

Weisskopf MG, Kioumourtzoglou M-A & Roberts AL, 'Air pollution and autism spectrum disorders: causal or confounded?' *Current Environmental Health Reports*, vol. 2, 23 September 2015, pp. 430–439.

Westmoquette M, *Mindful Thoughts for Stargazers: Find your inner universe*, Leaping Hare Press, 2 July 2019.

Westmoquette M, *The Mindful Universe: A journey through the inner and outer cosmos*, Leaping Hare Press, 15 September 2020.

White MP et al., 'Spending at least 120 minutes a week in nature is associated with good health and wellbeing'. *Scientific Reports*, vol. 9, no. 7730, 2019.

Whitworth E, 'Why did Thoreau go to the woods? 4 ways Walden drew him', *Shortform*, 30 November 2023, shortform.com/blog/why-did-thoreau-go-to-the-woods.

Wilson EO, *Biophilia: The human bond with other species*, Harvard University Press, 1986.

Wohlleben P, 'Engaging your senses in nature: exploring the value of touch', welldoing.org, 15 June 2021, welldoing.org/article/engaging-your-senses-in-nature-exploring-value-touch.

Woo CC et al., 'Overnight olfactory enrichment using an odorant diffuser improves memory and modifies the uncinate fasciculus in older adults', *Frontiers in Neuroscience*, vol. 17, 24 July 2023.

World Health Organization, 'Burn-out an "occupational phenomenon"', accessed 30 July 2024, who.int/standards/classifications/frequently-asked-questions/burn-out-an-occupational-phenomenon.

World Health Organization, 'Noncommunicable diseases', accessed 30 July 2024, who.int/data/gho/data/themes/noncommunicable-diseases.

World Health Organization Regional Office for Europe, *Burden of disease from environmental noise: quantification of health life years lost in Europe*, report, 2011, https://www.who.int/publications/i/item/9789289002295.

World Health Organization Regional Office for Europe, *Evolution of WHO Air Quality Guidelines: Past, present and future*, report, 1 October 2017, who.int/europe/publications/i/item/9789289052306.

World Health Organization Regional Office for Europe, *Green and Blue Spaces and Mental Health: New evidence and perspectives for action*, report, 2021, iris.who.int/bitstream/handle/10665/342931/9789289055666-eng.pdf.

World Health Organization, 'Health consequences of air pollution on populations', press release, 25 June 2024, who.int/news/item/15-11-2019-what-are-health-consequences-of-air-pollution-on-populations.

Wyles KJ et al., 'Are some natural environments more psychologically beneficial than others? The importance of type and quality on connectedness to nature and psychological restoration', *Environment and Behavior*, vol. 51, no. 2, 31 October 2017.

Xiong S et al., 'Time spent in outdoor activities in relation to myopia prevention and control: a meta-analysis and systematic review', *Acta Ophthalmologica*, vol. 95, no. 6, September 2017, pp. 551–566.

Xu L et al., 'Widespread receptor-driven modulation in peripheral olfactory coding', *Science*, vol. 368, no. 6487, 10 April 2020, eaaz5390.

Xu X et al., 'The contribution of raised blood pressure to all-cause and cardiovascular deaths and disability-adjusted life-years (DALYs) in Australia: analysis of global burden of disease study from 1990 to 2019', *PLOS ONE, vol. 19, no. 2, 21 February 2024, e0297229.*

Yamasaki S et al., 'Hot spring bathing is associated with a lower prevalence of hypertension among Japanese older adults: a cross-sectional study in Beppu', Scientific Reports, vol. 12, 14 November 2022, 19462.

Yang B-Y et al., 'Greenspace and human health: an umbrella review', *The Innovation*, vol. 2, no. 4, 28 November 2021, 100164.

Yang J, Chang Y & Yan, P, 'Ranking the suitability of common urban tree species for controlling PM2.5 pollution', *Atmospheric Pollution Research*, vol. 6, no. 2, March 2015.

Yankouskaya A et al., 'Short-term head-out whole-body cold-water immersion facilitates positive affect and increases interaction between large-scale brain networks', *Biology*, vol. 12, no. 2, 29 January 2023, 211.

References

Yeager RA, Smith TR & Bhatnagar A, 'Green environments and cardiovascular health', *Trends in Cardiovascular Medicine*, vol. 30, no. 4, May 2020, pp. 241–246.

Yoo O et al., 'Psychophysiological and emotional effects of human–dog interactions by activity type: an electroencephalogram study', *PLOS ONE*, vol. 19, no. 3, 13 March 2024, e0298384.

Zhang J et al., 'Weekly green space visit duration is positively associated with favorable health outcomes in people with hypertension: evidence from Shenzhen, China', *Environmental Research*, vol. 212, part B, September 2022, 113228.

Be better with business books

MAJOR STREET

We hope you enjoy reading this book. We'd love you to post a review on social media or your favourite bookseller site. Please include the hashtag #majorstreetpublishing.

Major Street Publishing specialises in business, leadership, personal finance and motivational non-fiction books. If you'd like to receive regular updates about new Major Street books, email info@majorstreet.com.au and ask to be added to our mailing list.

Visit majorstreet.com.au to find out more about our books (print, audio and ebooks) and authors, read reviews and find links to our Your Next Read podcast.

We'd love you to follow us on social media.

- linkedin.com/company/major-street-publishing
- facebook.com/MajorStreetPublishing
- instagram.com/majorstreetpublishing
- @MajorStreetPub

www.ingramcontent.com/pod-product-compliance
Lightning Source LLC
Chambersburg PA
CBHW010045090426
42735CB00020B/3395